ALL OUR LOVES

ALL OUR LOVES

*Journeys with Polyamory
in India*

ARUNDHATI GHOSH

ALEPH

ALEPH

ALEPH BOOK COMPANY
An independent publishing firm
promoted by *Rupa Publications India*

First published in India in 2025
by Aleph Book Company
7/16 Ansari Road, Daryaganj
New Delhi 110 002

ISBN: 978-93-6523-446-6

1 3 5 7 9 10 8 6 4 2

Printed in India

*for the patience of sarais
and lightness of musafirs—*

for lovers—lost, found, and let go

CONTENTS

Section III
Lighthouses in the Mist

STEPPING OUT, WADING IN: INTRODUCTION TO LOVES LIVED DIFFERENTLY

Unlike Emily Dickinson's 'hope', love is not 'a thing with feathers'. It has fangs and talons. It bites, it stings, it makes you want to end your life. And, it makes your life totally worth living, with all its dangerous, complex, seductive possibilities. In short, love is hard.

But love that attempts to cross boundaries is harder. Loving in ways that the world considers wrong could make one liable to suffer mental abuse, bodily harm, and even death. Anyone who has fallen in love with those socially declared as the 'wrong' gender, caste, colour, race, or religion, knows the price that has to be paid for such transgressions. As do those who have loved people from across borders, in enemy frontiers. And of course, queer people have been fighting through the decades for their right to love, under the banner of 'love is love'.

Yet polyamory—the practice, in my definition, of being in love with or without sexual intimacies with more than one person simultaneously, with the consent of all—is perhaps the last existing taboo. Even the most open-minded people I meet stumble when the singularity of love, monoamory—being in love with only one person at any given time—is challenged. Not just that, if there is a series of these single-partner relationships, they are all meant to culminate into the final 'one true love'. The adulation of singularity is doubled—first, with loving one person at a time, and then believing in only one true love after all! In our stories, films, songs, and poetry, there is a celebration of the longing, arrival, or loss of this one true love, sealing this singularity with a societal and often spiritual stamp that makes every other possibility of loving wrong, unethical, immoral, and altogether unacceptable.

But before we go any further, let me clarify that the definitions of polyamory and monoamory used in this book are different from polygamy and monogamy. While polyamory refers to loving many people simultaneously, the Greek word 'gamy' refers to marriage and so 'polygamy' means being married to many people. Similarly, monoamory is the practice of nurturing one relationship of love at a time, but monogamy means being married to one person. However, it is important to note that often monoamory and monogamy are used interchangeably. Also, more recently in popular culture, media, and other discourses, terms like ethical non-monogamy and consensual non-monogamy are being used interchangeably with polyamory, which is not correct. Polyamory is considered only one of the ways in which monoamory or monogamy can be challenged. For the purposes of this book I have mostly used the words monoamory and polyamory to refer to the two kinds of relationships of love, and resorted to monogamy and polygamy only when discussing systems of marriage.

MY OWN JOURNEY

I am fifty-one years old and have been in consensual relationships with more than one partner at a time over the past many years. I think it was in school in the late eighties that I first realized that I was capable of falling in love with more than one person. The only way I knew to cope was to end one relationship before starting another. That's what I had seen around me. For many years I was filled with self-loathing, thinking of myself as a shallow, fickle, and unstable person unable to build anything longer-term. There was also the fear of people getting to know about these feelings that I had. It was my friend Kaushik with whom I had my first discussion about this, when I was in my twenties. By then, he was openly polyamorous. He asked me to read *The Ethical Slut: A Guide to Infinite Sexual Possibilities* (1997) written by Dossie Easton and Janet Hardy. It was a guide for single people and couples to have multiple ethical and emotionally sustainable relationships. Kaushik was living in the US at that time and knew people who were practising polyamory. He engaged with their non-traditional families comprising three or four partners who shared emotional, romantic, and sexual relations as well as parenting responsibilities. The book was a revelation.

While some of the ignorance and doubts I had about my feelings cleared, I was filled with new questions. Was this even practical to pursue? Were there people like me in India? Given the tight-hold that the traditional family has over people here, would it be possible for polyamory to exist openly? Born into a mixed-caste love-marriage of the mid-sixties, I had experienced what transgressive love could do to people. I had seen my parents go through ostracization and abuse by their families. No matter how much they attempted to protect me, I was singed as well. With no extended family, the loneliness bit into my skin. Crossing caste boundaries was already protected by law—yet it was traumatic. I wondered what horrors would be unleashed on polyamorous people if they were to express themselves openly. The queer movement was still not quite visible in India, and I had nothing to compare notes with. In India, 'one true love' is sanctioned in marriage in most religions, making it a sacred bond. Hindus claim holy unions last through seven lifetimes of couples, while Catholic Christianity prohibits divorce. I wondered how sinful polyamory would be considered in this country! However, one thing was clear to me: I most certainly had the desire and the ability to love more than one person at a time, with the hope of building lasting relationships. It was after much reading and speaking with kindred souls that I came out—accepted my being, and felt comfortable talking about it.

BRINGING IT INTO THE PUBLIC DOMAIN

In the beginning, when I tried bringing up polyamory as a topic of conversation among people, I noticed that the talks were, at best, uncomfortable and at worst, sleazy. There is curiosity but people are unable to express it without sounding perverse. They assume polyamory to entail only a series of indiscriminate and mindless sexual activities, and want to know only about the sex. What is the fear, I wondered, that lies at the core of this hesitation to take it seriously. Is it because it crumbles the idea of the family as we know it? Is it because it ruptures economic models of existence through collective living? Makes it impossible for the state to control its citizens? Or has it more to do with our own insecurities and worries about being replaced, deserted, unloved? I realized that while no one questions a mother's instinct and ability to love all her children, there is grave suspicion around loving more than one person romantically and sexually.

But I am fortunate. Over the years, I have met many people who have more than one love in their lives, often blurring the conventional boundaries between friendship and romance. Some do not believe in the boundaries created by privileges of sex and romance that dictate the hierarchies of relationships. Still others refuse to participate in relationship ecologies that make it mandatory to make choices between people they love. Some identify as being polyamorous and some choose not to label themselves. Some agree with the broader accepted frameworks that guide polyamory and some have their own ways of breaking rules. Life is being lived around this country in a myriad ways—testing, struggling, challenging, and disrupting conventional ways of being. Some quietly, some not so much. Various kinds of political and ideological explorations like socialism, feminism, and queer thoughts have led to enquiries into the oppressive legacy of the patriarchal heteronormative family structure. While there are still fewer people willing to discuss polyamory in the public domain, I know the numbers are on the rise.

When I started writing about my own insights and struggles with polyamory a few years ago on social media, the responses were heartening. Except for some who called me a slut or sent me abusive messages, most were patient and curious to listen to the different points of view. Soon, people started sharing their stories with me, invited me to write articles for publications, and organized conversations on the topic. I found a support group, Bangalore Polycule, and met some incredible people who have been practising polyamory against all odds. It has been a collective expedition of learning.

WHY THIS BOOK

The journey of this book started with some people questioning my need to write about polyamory on social media. They are not people who think polyamory is wrong for whatever reasons. I am talking about friends who agreed with me about polyamory being a valid way of loving and living. Their argument was: since this was not something new, why the sudden fuss around it? 'It was always there,' they said. 'Only now it's become a fad with all this song and dance around it.' Some others said that love and relationships were private matters and did not need discussions in public. Still others felt too much conversation around love would take away its essence, its mojo. Love loses its ethereality, its transcendental powers, its magic, if it is categorized, named, defined. 'Pyar ko pyar hi rehne do, koi naam na do (Let love be love, don't give it a name),' croons Lata Mangeshkar in *Khamoshi* (1968).

Some of that is true. And I would agree to not writing about love at all if only love was not one of the key reasons why people are discriminated against across the world. Until recently, people have been criminalized for love in India; in many other countries they still are. They are denied equal status and rights that all citizens should have. Love is a political struggle. While the Preamble of our Constitution gives us the power of freedom of expression, society judges love harshly. Therefore, love that breaks rules, and is made invisible by derision and denial, must be put out there, discussed, and written about—as loudly and frequently as possible. Also, like one would say about writing for any minority group's right to be and thrive, one needs to write about polyamory so others understand why we are who we are.

That's where my argument for making this book began. But soon I realized there were other reasons, just as compelling. I wanted to dispel the idea that monoamory was the only natural, ethical, and harmonious way to live. I wanted to bust the prevalent misconceptions about polyamorous people. I wanted to share what life could look like if only we questioned the various assumptions about love. I had been misunderstood for a long time, trying to adjust to a monoamorous world. It was a struggle for me to accept and celebrate myself. I knew there were others out there feeling as rejected, as forlorn. I wanted them to feel less lost, less lonely, knowing we are many more.

What is particularly important for my readers to understand is that this book is not about trashing monoamory. I have great respect for people who love, be it any kind of love. I have a problem with monoamory only when it proclaims to be the sole correct way to love and live. The book is also not about proving that being polyamorous is a better, tougher, sexier, or cooler way to be. All it attempts to do is share from a slightly different perspective that love is difficult and glorious at the same time, no matter whom or how many people we love. The challenges, the heartbreaks, the loneliness, and the fear remain the same, no matter what kind of love we decide to invoke in our lives. And yet, in all its fragility and suffering, it still remains one of the few dazzling reasons to be alive.

A more practical argument for this book is the fact that, until recently, we had access to experiences of polyamory only in the Western world. The books written by people in the West living polyamorous lives, courageous as they are, illuminated the journeys in contexts and conditions very different from our post-colonial, multicultural environment. India is as messy as it is breathtaking. Families here exert far more influence on individual lives, as do communities held tightly together within boundaries of class, caste, and religion. Social conditioning is amplified with justifications of tradition and culture. While the liberation movements around caste, class, gender, sexuality, and minority rights become stronger each day, much of our lives are still mired in the oppression of those identities. This context is unique to this land, and thus to the lived experiences of polyamory here. That's why there needed to be a book that was written from here, about this place.

WHO THIS BOOK IS FOR

This book is for different kinds of people, I do hope. For polyamorous people like me, who have for the longest time felt invisible, I hope this book is solidarity from a fellow traveller. It does not want to set standard practices or guidelines to polyamory but intends only to celebrate it in all its dynamic shapes and eccentricities with you. For those who have questions about the practice from within it, I hope the conversations and insights here help you find your own adventure. For those who are monoamorous but have polyamorous partners, may this book help you understand your partner and their heart better. For those who are thinking about opening up to polyamorous lives, I wish it introduces you to the joys as well as the hardships, so you choose what is best for you. For those who have been monoamorous but struggle to stay within its limits, I promise this book will present other options. And finally, for those who are just curious to find out why some people live differently, I hope it delights you.

STRUCTURE OF THE BOOK

I love the ocean. Covering over 70 per cent of our home planet, life itself was generated in the ocean. I am fascinated by its infinite expanse, its fathomless depth, and the multitudes of enchanting life forms that it sustains. I feel enthralled by its many moods and mysteries, so much so that I am sure I was a sailor in some ancient life. While land on this world as we know it has been mapped, owned, conquered, and ravaged—much of our oceans still remains uncharted, with secret universes enveloped in its darkness. Most of all, what I love about the ocean is that no one owns it. The 'freedom of the seas' doctrine, a seventeenth-century principle, limits the rights and jurisdiction of a country only over a thin belt of the ocean surrounding it. The rest of the oceans and seas are free for all as global commons. Exploring polyamory, for me, has been akin to leaving the known, owned land of relationships and entering the freedom of the ocean. That's why this introduction to the book is entitled 'Stepping out, Wading in' and the book is divided into the following three sections.

The first section entitled 'The Shape of the Ocean' is an effort to understand the scope of polyamory. The chapters in this section deal with a quest across the world for non-monogamous cultures, misconceptions about polyamorous people, and the various ways in which contemporary polyamory is lived in India.

The second section entitled 'Sailing with Many Loves' focuses on the various aspects of the actual practice of polyamory. Here, the chapters comprise discussions on the cornerstones of the practice—honesty and consent—and the elephant in the room—jealousy, the choice of living as a solo polyamorous person, the difficulties of the practice, steps to begin exploring, and the misuse and abuse of the practice.

The third section entitled 'Lighthouses in the Mist' attempts to bring together conversations on the ecology within which polyamory is practised. Here the chapters shed light on the legal concerns and access to support systems through interviews with experts in those fields. The last chapter deals with the making of a new language around polyamory and lists a range of words with their definitions.

Among these chapters are inserts that I call 'Boat(s) of Hope'. These are little, luminescent vessels floating around in the ocean of polyamory—people who have talked to me about their lives. They are from various walks of life, both straight and queer, exploring and experimenting with love. The conversations, retained in their voices, are my attempt to infuse in this book the spirit of pulsating life in all its raw, uncensored, and passionate energy.

While many of the insights of this book come from my own living as a continuously faltering, yet evolving and hopeful polyamorous person, some are from my partners and friends whom I have intimately seen struggle through many definitions of love. There is also plenty here that comes from people I have had the privilege to know as openly or privately polyamorous. While for a chapter in this book I have used assisted research, my own years of reading and connecting with communities and platforms that support polyamorous people have also contributed to this book's making.

AND SOME POINTS TO NOTE

My experiences have been mostly within heterosexual relationships, so my insights are from that perspective. Polyamory has many more stories from other genders and sexualities. Also, most of my conversations with polyamorous people have been in cities, within the educated middle and upper middle class, and in the languages of English, Bangla, and Hindi. I know there are several other worlds of polyamory in places I have not been to, among people I have not met, in languages I have no skills in, and contexts I am unfamiliar with. Those stories remain unheard, and the voices unaccounted for. Therefore, in no way is this book either exhaustive or inclusive of all the myriad depths of the ocean that polyamory is. It is only an attempt to share a few journeys from that immense expanse.

THE SHAPE OF THE OCEAN

As if the Sea should part
And show a further Sea—
And that—a further—and the Three
But a presumption be—

Of Periods of Seas—
Unvisited of Shores—
Themselves the Verge of Seas to be—
Eternity—is Those—

—Emily Dickinson

1

THE WORLD WITH MORE: IN SEARCH OF NON-MONOGAMOUS CULTURES

Since monoamory is exalted as the only ethical and moral way to love and live, monogamy is seen as the norm in our societies. But the connection between 'amour', or love, and 'gamy', or marriage, is tenuous and more recent than we think. Marriage itself is one of the oldest institutions around, with the first recorded one in Mesopotamia in 2350 BCE. But the purpose was quite different. Those marriages were alliances that were historically forged on the basis of many factors that included accumulation and safeguard of power and private property, creating controlled patriarchal structures for procreation, and building networks of kinship for protection from enemies. Love had very little to do with it. So, one might wonder why I begin a book about contemporary polyamory with a search for non-monogamous cultures. The reason is that in the contemporary world of relationships, we have conflated love with marriage or partnerships, and the normative conditions of monoamory and monogamy—loving one person at a time and being married to one person at a time—strengthen each other's existence and justification. Thus, it made sense to go on this exploration of non-monogamous cultures across the world to understand the range and diversity of being in relationships of love, desire, marriage, and 'family', with more than one person. It is also a way of saying, 'Hey,' and quoting Billy Joel, 'We didn't start the fire. It was always burning, since the world's been turning.'

These non-monogamous practices encompass different ways of defying monogamy. While polygamy—both polyandry, where one woman has more than one husband, and polygyny, where one man has more than one wife—is included, there are also socially approved systems of taking on more than one partner or lover outside of marital arrangements. In many communities, multiple practices, very different from each other, coexist, creating fluidity of choice and various patterns of relationships. Having grown up in a heteronormative monogamous family system in a moderately conservative home, it was often difficult for me to get my head around the sheer diversity of possibilities that the research threw up! But while contemporary polyamory varies in many ways from these cultures that I came across, there was great learning in the differences of value systems and priorities, the scope and dimensions of relationships, and the alternative approaches to living that they had to offer.

There is abundant research on non-monogamous cultures from across the world. However, most of these studies in South America, Asia, and Africa, have been conducted by Western anthropologists viewing through the lens of the heteronormative monogamous nuclear family of the West. These cultures are also judged by Western standards of morality. For example, I noticed that in the case of polyandrous cultures, it is often argued that the only reasons for their existence are skewed sex ratio, female infanticide, and distribution of land resources, reducing them to mere functional purposes that suit predisposed biases of Western logic. Also, one must note that in many of these cultures the locus of power is never at one single point within the family like in heteronormative monogamous structures, where it rests with the father figure. The power dynamics among the various players and their negotiations can be much more layered and complicated. No doubt some non-monogamous practices suffer from unequal power equations and sexism—but it is difficult to say whether that is any more or less than what is present within heteronormative monogamy.

However, this exercise is in no way an attempt to prove one system inherently better than another. Instead, the effort is to point to the existence, in most cases till quite recently, of a vast range of systems in the world. Given the limited scope of this book, I have only initiated very brief introductions to some of these cultures and practices to offer openings for readers to make their own explorations of non-monogamous societies if they are interested. This list chosen here, based on existing research and studies, is not exhaustive and reflects only my own levels of curiosity when I came across them.

POLYANDRY

Among the various non-monogamous practices that exist, polygyny—where one man has more than one wife—is more prevalent and commonly understood. It has become almost synonymous with polygamy. Therefore, let us begin exploring from the other end—the various polyandrous communities where women have more than one husband or partner. Here are some fascinating examples:

The Bari of Venezuela: Women of the Bari community in Venezuela have great agency in making choices, and are liberated sexually from a young age. They can freely mate with anyone as long as they do not cross the incest taboo. This community relies mainly on horticulture in the lowland tropical rainforest. While marriages here are mostly monogamous, women often have multiple relationships with men outside of marriage. Married men can also be secondary husbands to other women. The community believes that a child can have more than one biological father and thus practise what is known as partible paternity. This means that all the men who have been in a sexual relationship with a woman a couple of months before her pregnancy are named secondary husbands and considered the father of the child. This system of paternity and flexible family structure ensures that the child has additional protection and insurance from multiple male parents with obligation and responsibility to look after the child. The stringent sexual restrictions women in our modern societies cope with simply to ensure paternity seem even more ludicrous in comparison!

The Ache of Paraguay: Among the Ache community of Paraguay, a tribe practising small-scale horticulture and living as hunters and gatherers until the 1980s, a husband and a wife can take on one more partner each, and all four of them live together. That's what I call a house on fire! Like the Bari, the Ache also believe in partible paternity where the child grows up with shared fatherhood. At birth, the mother names all the men she has been with, who are the fathers of the child. This opens the community to more resources and access to sexual alliances.

The Irigwe of Nigeria: Among the Irigwe tribe of the Jos Plateau of Northern Nigeria, the first marriage of a couple is arranged at a young age where parents decide their partners. Later, the woman can take on more husbands, and even after she has children, she can decide how much legitimacy to give each partner. Talk about women in charge! Unlike practices in some other communities where polyandry is restricted to the brothers of the first husband, in this community, non-fraternal relationships are preferred. The woman can have children with any of her husbands and also choose whom to live with. These multiple marriages bring many families from different groups together through their relationship with one woman. A man can also marry multiple times, but while husbands are all treated equally, the first wife has a more important place in society.

The Marquesan of the Pacific: The practice of polyandry among the inhabitants of the Marquesas Islands in French Polynesia in the central South Pacific Ocean region consists of households having two or three husbands for one wife. That would swing between a lot of help and a lot to handle! There is a main or primary husband who is called vahana haka'iki and all children of the wife are considered to be his. Secondary husbands taken later are called peiko. Often, the lovers of a woman from her younger days join her as peikos when she gets married to a primary husband. Initially, this was a practice only among the elite. The non-elite were either monogamous or entered affluent households as peikos for sustenance. Even after sexual relations ended, peikos could remain in their positions. Sometimes, men too would take on second wives who joined the household.

The Nyinba of Nepal: The Nyinba is an agro-pastoral tribe that lives on the northwestern border of Nepal in the Humla district, who also engage in trade. While various kinds of marriages are prevalent, fraternal polyandry is the most dominant and preferred type of marriage among them, where a woman marries all the brothers. The tribe is patrilineal, and women do not inherit land or property. While property and children are registered with the dag-pa or the male head who is generally the oldest brother, the dag-ma—the wife—has access to all trade relations and must always be consulted before decision-making. She is the centre of the household. Usually, only the dag-pa is present in the house most times as the other brothers are away for months trading or sheep herding. However, he cannot monopolize sexual or emotional intimacy with the wife. The wife is responsible for equal access and strategically divides time among the husbands. Sexual practices in the tribe are also very liberal with free mixing and relationships developing among people from young ages. There is also the practice of long-term committed relationships outside of marriages. There are matchmakers for this practice too, and often all parties are cognizant of the situation. That's a matchmaker's resume I would love to read!

The Mosuo of China: The Mosuo community who live in the border regions of the Sichuan and Yunnan provinces of the Himalayan region of China are often called the last matrilineal society. Property such as land, or money, is controlled by a female head and handed down to their daughters. Fully insured streedhan! While men can also act as temporary custodians, their rights have to be transferred to their sister's children. Traditionally, the concept of fatherhood does not exist for them. This sets the precedent for sese or walking marriages, where, upon reaching puberty, girls can take on lovers who visit them at night but live in separate households. There is no formal contract between partners and women may have multiple lovers throughout their lifetime. Since paternity is not important, biological fathers seldom participate in child-rearing. The mother's brother is often the father figure for the child.

The Nairs of Kerala, the tribes of Jaunsar Bawar in Uttarakhand, and the Lachenpas of Sikkim in India: In India, too, there are a few communities that practised polyandry till recently or continue to do so. The most well-known are the Nairs, the matrilineal sub-caste group in Kerala, who did not, till the 1920s, have the concept of monogamous marriage in their community. Women lived in matrilineal households where parentage and lineage were traced through the mother. There was a mock marriage ritual set up for a girl upon reaching the appropriate age but the husband immediately left for his house after the marriage and the woman observed formal mourning. After this, she was free to choose lovers. Similar to the sese or walking marriage system in the Mosuo community in China, lovers of a woman could visit her with gifts but did not live with her. And similar to the Mosuo, the maternal uncle was an important figure in the household. Different sub-groups of Nairs in different regions had varying forms of this system of relationship.

Several tribes among the people who live in the Jaunsar Bawar region in the Dehradun district of Uttarakhand in the central Himalayas practise polyandry. Some of them consider the Pandavas from the Mahabharata to be their ancestors. In the epic, princess Draupadi was married to the five Pandava brothers. The tribes follow the same practice of fraternal polyandry, which is known as the Pandava Pratha or the tradition of the Pandavas.

The Lachenpas, the inhabitants of the Lachung valley in North Sikkim, are agro-pastoralists and landowners. Though they are a patrilineal community with political power in the hands of the male elders, women in Lachung Valley generally have agency over their sexuality and in socio-cultural matters. While multiple marital forms are present in this community, polyandry is historically more prevalent.

POLYGYNY

Polygyny is a common form of polygamy among non-monogamous arrangements around the world. There are many examples from across time, cultures, and continents. While each system has its own distinctive features, most follow a broad, common definition and similar practices. There are many countries in Asia and Africa where polygyny is still legal. Wherever the law has made it illegal, it is still not considered a criminal activity. For this book, I tried to understand the journey of polygyny in India.

Studies state that historically, polygyny was a practice that was common in India among the elite, the aristocrats, and many tribal communities. It is not possible to draw a uniform trajectory about the evolution of the practices across the diverse and geographically widespread cultures in the country, but it did exist in different forms under various circumstances in regions across India. During the Indus Valley Civilizations (3300 BCE–1300 BCE), it is believed that monarchs had several wives. It is also believed that in the Vedic period (1500 BCE–600 BCE), while monogamy was more common, the ruling classes practised polygyny and a husband could take a second wife under certain circumstances. Polygyny was also permissible during the Mughal rule and aristocrats like the Rajputs were known to marry multiple women for political alliances. However, under the colonial rule, legal provisions were made to limit polygyny. The Indian Penal Code of 1860 makes polygamy (and thereby polygyny) a punishable offence except for those following Islam, since under Islamic law a man can have up to four wives if he is able to give them shelter. The Christian Marriage Act of 1872 also declared polygamous marriages invalid. Post-Independence, the Hindu Marriage Act of 1955 legally abolished polygamy for all Hindu communities. The Special Marriage Act of 1954 allows individuals to perform inter-religious marriages, but that too forbids polygamy. Yet, the National Family Health Survey (NFHS) of 2019–20 states that polygyny continues to be prevalent across India among various groups.

UNIQUE SYSTEMS

The Bulsa of Ghana and Lovedu of South Africa: Among the many intriguing non-monogamous practices that I read about, studies on two unique ones fascinated me. The first is from the Bulsa community in Northern Ghana. They have a polygynous society where a man has many wives. But there are two types of relationships between a married woman and a man outside of her marriage, which have the consent of her husband and approval of society.

In the first case, if the husband is old or unable to have children, the wife is allowed a sexual relationship with another man who can provide her with children. In the second case a romantic, emotional, and totally non-sexual relationship called the pok nong is allowed between a married woman and a man outside of her marriage. This man is her boyfriend, or nong, who often acts as an arbitrator in conflicts that happen between her and her husband and gives her emotional support when she needs it. The husband is fully aware and must approve of the relationship. When the boyfriend visits the wife, the husband cuts a fowl and the wife gives the boyfriend a feast. Sometimes, the boyfriend stays the night and sleeps in the husband's room, sharing a mat with the wife. No sexual intimacy is allowed between them and he leaves at dawn. The wife is also given the responsibility to find her nong a wife from their own community. This boyfriend and the husband are often linked through kinship or lineage, strengthening relationships within the clan.

The other practice is among the Lovedu tribe from the northern province of South Africa. They are a Bantu-speaking community whose kinship, politics, economy, and religion are centred in their Rain Queen, or Modjajdi, who is believed to have come from divine ancestors. She used to take on many women as wives who were offered as tributes from different regions in her kingdom. She acted as the female head of her family of many wives. That would have been a different kind of harem! For procreation, a male called boho, or bull, was appointed, but he was not part of the marriage or the household. The Modjajdi was succeeded by either her daughter, or the daughter of one of her wives. This system was emulated by common folk too, where a woman who did not have a son could take on wives. Women in the Lovedu clan could also have the right to their earnings after marriage through the practice of bride-wealth. As Christianity became more prevalent among the tribe, its impact made many of the older traditions untenable. In 1959, for the first time, the Rain Queen married a man.

INTENTIONAL COMMUNITIES PRACTISING NON-MONOGAMY

In addition to the non-monogamous cultures of these communities, there are also collectives and groups that were set up intentionally over time in various parts of the world, with the idea of loving differently from the heteronormative monogamous ways of society. Though each was mired in its own complications and problems, they still broke many conventions of society and established path-breaking ways of living. Here are a few of the ones I found intriguing:

The Oneida in New York, US: The Oneida community in New York, started by John Humphrey in 1848, is one of the few examples in history of a community based on a polyamorous system. While some studies proclaim Humphrey as a saviour of women, more recent feminist readings conclude that he was a male chauvinist who disappointed the people in the community seeking equality. Despite this, the community was an example of how group marriage could be practised among consenting adults. Property and other possessions in this community belonged to the group and not to individuals. They also practised mutual group criticism and male continence, where men voluntarily avoided sexual climax, as a way of learning. The community of about 300 members lived together like a family in a mansion called the Manor House. All adult members were considered married to each other and consensual sexual relations were permitted. Some accounts show that older women often initiated young men to sex, which has been seen as a problematic power dynamic by some scholars.

The Kerista in New York, US: The Kerista commune was founded in New York City in 1956 by John Peltz Presmont. Kerista has two distinct periods of history: the Old Tribe and the New Tribe. The Old Tribe was a loosely organized communal movement with people living in clusters across different apartments in New York. Sex among them was free, open-ended, and unregulated. The New Tribe began about fifteen years later when a communal loft was bought and used by about thirty members at a time. This was a more organized community with a large set of rules that included people maintaining fidelity within the group. This system, also called the B-FIC—best friend identity cluster—included twenty to forty partners who were faithful to each other and slept with each other on a fixed rotating schedule. They also had a process called 'gestalt-o-rama', where in-depth face-to-face criticism could be done in a group. While reading about many of these practices, I realized that being able to accept and learn from criticism was common among many groups. I wonder if that was part of a process to control personal egos so that people could live together harmoniously. If so, perhaps we should bring that back into practice in our lives. The New Tribe had more of an atmosphere of a cult and it ultimately disbanded after internal conflicts in 1991.

The Komaja in Switzerland: Komaja, meaning 'radiant love', is a contemporary community in Gersau, Switzerland, founded in 1978 by Aba Aziz Makaja. He developed a specific form of tantric kundalini yoga and is the spiritual leader at the centre of this community. Komaja is also the spiritual and philosophical knowledge system that is practised by the 300 members of the community spread across the world. They consider this knowledge as the spiritual thread connecting them and radiant love, their principal virtue. The members of the community practise zajedna, which is a spiritual and psychic union between at least two or more people. If one of the members of this group falls in love with a new person, that person may join the zajedna. Sexual intimacy is not central to the system but a person who does not connect sexually with the members of zajedna cannot do so with others outside the group either. When any of the members have children, all of them participate in raising the child. Leaving the zajedna is frowned upon and considered abandoning the spiritual path.

The Church of All Worlds, California, US: The Church of All Worlds (CAW) has been described as a neo-pagan group based in Cotati, California, founded in 1961. The CAW evolved from a group of friends and lovers who were inspired by the fictional religion that Robert Heinlein created in his novel *Stranger in a Strange Land*. Oberon Zell-Ravenheart (formerly Timothy Zell) is one of the key founders of the CAW. Over the years, it has grown beyond its sci-fi roots, adopting belief systems and practices that have integrated it into the modern pagan movement. It is now a community that embraces a polyamorous lifestyle. They believe that individuals should feel comfortable practising it and they share all their feelings, including discomfort. For them, these relationships constitute making commitments and taking responsibilities for the people they love and build lives with. However, the community allows people to decide for themselves whether they would choose polyamory or remain with one partner.

Rajneesh and the Osho movement: The movement started by Rajneesh in the 1970s in India, known as the Osho movement, is perhaps one of the most well-known and widely followed spiritual movements in the recent history of the world where free love was propagated. The movement was defined as a space for spiritual enlightenment and sexual liberation. Rajneesh encouraged individuals to forgo the institution of marriage and live together under the principles of free love. It later spread to Oregon in the US, where it faced hostility from the locals due to its belief in open marriages, free love and sex, and support for contraception and abortion. This was followed by a series of controversial allegations against it. While its history is contentious, some of the most interesting ideas from the Rajneesh movement about spiritual and free love challenged the mainstream system of heteronormative family and religion.

The Tamera: Based in Portugal, Tamera is a community of about 160 people, founded in 1978. Their mission is to create a new world, Terra Nova, by working towards autonomous decentralized models for a post-capitalist world. The community seeks a future without war, and love without fear. They attempt to do this by building what they call 'healing biotopes'. These are learning centres that attempt to bring together the world we are given and the world we want to make so that through trust, faith, and effort the wounds of the former can be healed. While the community does not label itself as polyamorous, many teachings of its Love School focus on a kind of love that is free of jealousy. This aligns them with similar beliefs of other contemporary non-monogamous communities. Tamera's values leave space for people to have other relationships while they have a partner, to have erotic friendships and encounters, or to be monogamous. They also have no rules about sexual choices or orientation.

These cultures give us a sense of the enormous array of alternative life and love styles that the world has experienced. Yet, since most of us have grown up in heteronormative monogamous societies in nuclear or partially extended families, we experience monogamy as the only possible practice. Anything outside of that is considered abnormal if not unimaginable. The evolution of human cohabitation, marriage, procreating, and nurturing of offspring has a complex and layered narrative that is influenced by the various histories of religion, invasion, patriarchy, and changes in economic and political systems. However, it is important to understand at least some of the key factors as explained by scholars, as to why monogamy developed as a dominant practice over time. These are neither exhaustive nor conclusive but do shed light on a large spectrum of possible reasons.

EVOLUTION OF MONOGAMY AS THE DOMINANT PRACTICE

There are several speculations on why monogamy became the predominant form of marriage and romantic relationship around the world. The biological and anthropological explanations try to establish that this was natural for humans. However, most of these theories today are severely challenged by newer studies. Contrary to the former view, historical explanations point to monogamy being a social construct built over time. With the advent of private property and questions of inheritance, monogamy developed as a social agreement to organize family labour and gender roles, define property rights, and ascertain lineage for inheritance. And then, monogamy became the more dominant form of marriage as westernization reached various parts of the world through the spread of Christianity and colonization. In many parts of the world, polygamy in the forms of polyandry and polygyny as well as other practices of non-monogamy in various forms were illegalized when the colonial powers established themselves in those lands.

BIOLOGICAL AND ANTHROPOLOGICAL EXPLANATIONS

There is a range of deterministic biological and anthropological theories that explain monogamy to be natural in humans. However, the notion that science and scientific methods are objective is itself problematic. Like most knowledge systems, biological and anthropological sciences are entrenched in Euro-centric perspectives and assumptions. Angela Willey notes in *Undoing Monogamy* (2016), that the emergence of biological science and anthropology in European history happened around the same time as colonial conquest and black slavery began, making these sciences prejudiced about race, sexuality, and what they found outside of Europe. She also points to the attempt at proving monogamy to be 'natural' through science, based on the assumption that evolution of humans progressed in a linear way from promiscuity to patriarchal monogamy—a theory put out by Lewis Henry Morgan. These archaic theories are being strongly refuted in the postcolonial world.

Science also relied on the behavioural patterns of other animals to study monogamy. However, research shows that early notions of such monogamy—for example, in birds—have been challenged in later studies. Even penguins, often celebrated for their apparent monogamy, engage only in ecologically imposed monogamy, forming new pair bonds each mating season.

A significant explanation of monogamy revolves around parental care. However, while the extended period of dependence of children on their parents justifies the necessity for both parents to stay in a long-term relationship, the existence of alternative caregiving structures of broader family networks and communities have added complexity and interrogated this theory. Closely linked to this proposition is the phenomenon of 'male mate guarding', where the male guards the mother and their offspring from rival males seeking to mate with the female and kill the child. However, the assertion that paternal care drove monogamy is challenged since empirical data reveals that over 40 per cent of socially monogamous species exhibit no indications of male care. All we need to understand that finding is to look at care structures and roles in our own families. Also, it is argued that parental care can be substituted by communal child rearing. The proverb 'it takes a village to raise a child' that came out of various African cultures, which shared strong non-monogamous histories, wasn't created in a hurry.

It has also been suggested that ecological factors, including the prevalence of sexually transmitted infections and scarcity of partners, could have played a role in favouring the development of monogamous relationships.

SOCIAL AND HISTORICAL EXPLANATIONS

According to some studies, the monogamous family system might have emerged in Europe around the Neolithic Age, with the advent of agriculture, land, and property. Moving from a wandering to a more settled lifestyle, land and property became important for agricultural and farming societies. Ownership of property had an important impact on human civilization. The need for passing on property to heirs necessitated for women to not have more than one husband to bear children with. While polygyny persisted, monogamy started to gain currency slowly. This also affected gendered labour within families.

Among the early cultures, the Greco-Roman civilization was one of the first to practise socially sanctioned monogamy through marriage. The rules were that a man could only have one wife, but he was allowed to engage in sexual activity with other women. The inheritance went from the father to the first-born son of the wife. Daughters or other children, or those born out of wedlock, did not have any rights. This system helped to concentrate power only in the hands of a few families. Greco-Roman monogamy's key role was in shaping Christian, and later, Western marital standards that became dominant across the world.

The Christian church played a significant role in countering polygamous trends across the countries and cultures it travelled to and reinforced Greco-Roman monogamy. The Bible connects idolatry and unfaithfulness. Robert Alter in his book *The Five Books of Moses: A Translation with Commentary* (2004) observed that the concept of monogamy is used metaphorically to represent monotheism, and worshipping other deities is likened to infidelity or promiscuity. As monogamy expanded through Christianization, the church also grappled with challenges related to divorce and the practice of elite concubines. It regulated these practices to strengthen monogamy, and developed elaborate ideological frameworks to promote it, while encouraging sexual restraint.

With the rise of colonization that further supported Christian missions logistically and morally, the direct attack on non-monogamous ways of living increased. With the spread of Western power, socially imposed monogamy began spreading across different cultures. People were encouraged and coerced to become monogamous with the justification that it was aligned and compatible with Christian values, more civilized, and less harmful for women. In most of these cultures, any way of being outside of heterosexual monogamy was quickly outlawed.

Friedrich Engels argued that the nuclear family structure arose during the rise of capitalism, forming an important aspect of capitalist relations of production. He emphasized that the origin of this monogamous family lies in economic conditions when societies moved from primitive communism, where land and resources were owned collectively, to the dominance of private ownership of property and thus the need for identifying legitimate heirs to pass on the inheritance. This enabled the rich families to keep their wealth within the family and maintain social inequality. This was achieved through monogamy and the oppression of women and their sexuality. This tyrannical family structure was not just monogamous but also heterosexual.

In *The Subjugation of Women Under Capitalism: The Bourgeois Morality* (1977), Marlene Dixon observes the discrepancy between the moral rationale for enforcing monogamy and fidelity, and its actual purpose. She explains that while the husband's supposed concern is determining his fatherhood through monogamy, it is actually about commanding his control over the labour and reproductive capacity of his wife. Children were prized assets for labour and establishing paternity was essential for husbands to assert ownership over this labour too. Monogamy served to fix and bind a woman to one man, making her his possession. It would guard against anyone 'stealing' her, and protect his authority over both her labour and the labour of their children.

These are just some of the explanations offered as to why monogamy over time became the most prevalent way of being. For way too long, the only image of the ideal family has been a monogamous, heterosexual, patriarchal, and nuclear one with gendered roles. Today, the singularity of that image is being challenged by scholars and activists to present diverse, queer, and feminist families. In similar spirit, monogamy, too, should be challenged as the only tenable form of partnership, making way for sustainable and nurturing polyamorous rainbow families. After all, with progressive discourse building around decolonization, monogamy in this diverse land of the *Kamasutra* cannot remain unquestioned.

2

STANDING TRIAL: BELIEFS AND MISCONCEPTIONS

Even though non-monogamous cultures were spread across the world, and monogamy was only socially constructed for various historical reasons, today, society puts on trial people who are polyamorous for our supposedly non-conformist choice. There are several beliefs about love, and misconceptions about the practice of polyamory, that make it difficult to begin any serious conversation about any relationships other than those which adhere to monoamorous values. So, before I discuss what contemporary polyamory is, I thought it best to get out of the way what it is not. That will clear the path, through the rest of the book, for us to concentrate on the expansive possibilities of all the things it is, and can be. This is a bit like clarifying on a dating profile who you are not. That would save potential dates their failed expectations or rude judgments of you later on, and allow them to enjoy your company for who you really are.

There is a set of fundamental beliefs about relationships which has been constructed and consolidated over time, fortifying the idea of monoamory, rationalizing its existence and perpetuating its practice. It is quite clear that the current family structure is facing a crisis. With depression, alienation, violence, abuse, and self-harm, things are falling apart and the centre is not holding anymore (salaam to Yeats). Yet, monoamory, with all its bells and whistles, is propped up with the aid of these beliefs, as the only correct way to be. Some of these beliefs are as follows:

BELIEFS THAT SUPPORT MONOAMORY

One true love: 'There is only one true love per lifetime.' The rest are attributed to lesser emotions and termed flings, infatuations, affairs. They are emptied out of whatever significance they possess in order that, in comparison, the one true love shines brightly. Not unlike the dance sequences in Indian films where less glamorous dancers are chosen to make the heroine look the most stunning. The one true love is put in the spotlight while all others are mistakes and misadventures. The goal is to search for and find this one true love and once acquired, hold on to it for dear life. Losing it is seen as the greatest tragedy from which one most certainly must never recover! I have often felt suffocated listening to the paeans of the one true love across popular culture—songs, stories, and films—and the utter waste of lives where either such loves have not been found, or missed out, or lost.

Only monoamory leads to ethical sex: 'The only ethical way to have sex is in an exclusive twosome relationship.' While many societies and religions take a further step to restrict it within marriage, it is believed that any sexual encounter outside of the sacred twosome is immoral and sinful. It arouses shame, guilt, and self-loathing, and is hidden away as a dirty secret. Significant aspects of relationships, like loyalty, security, and trust are linked directly to this having or not having sex outside of the twosome. I have been witness to such secrets and stigma slowly eroding and destroying relationships. And every time I felt that a compassionate conversation and a different perspective could have really brought significantly better outcomes between two people who love each other.

Jealousy is desirable: 'Jealousy is not only a natural emotion but actually an important indicator of love.' Its existence is counted as evidence of love and often the amount of jealousy in a person is seen as directly proportional to the amount of love they have for their partner. It is even considered commendable and acts of violence committed under the excuse of jealousy are justified and offered some understanding. I remember how horribly scared I felt when I encountered for the first time an incident of acid being thrown on a young woman by her ex-lover who was jealous of her new boyfriend. This was treated with kindness by society, rather than with rage and a call for justice. The ire was built against the woman—how heartless of her to ditch him and move on! I felt unsafe in a world that encouraged such assaults. I also felt that my worth or lovability seemed to rest on how much toxic jealousy my relationships could produce.

The couple on top: 'The love of a couple is above all other kinds of love and relationships, be it between friends, family members, or siblings.' The hierarchy that this creates is responsible for phrases such as, 'No, we are not together. We are *just* friends.' I never understood why friendship compared to couplehood had to be shrunk and made apologetic, as irrelevant as 'just'. It is misleading and draws attention away from what friendship could actually be—vital and potent. The same world that produces justifications for monoamory also places every other relationship of camaraderie, care, and love as secondary to its purpose of creating the typical nuclear family structure of Hum Do Humare Do (we two, our two), as famously seen on family-planning posters of the 1980s in India. While other relationships are deemed less important than a couplehood, a single person is believed to be unfortunate and seen with pity. More recently, I realized how children are conditioned into such prejudice through refrains like 'one for sorrow, two for joy' when looking out for those little brown birds for luck. Simply put, this means that a single bird is supposed to be sad and lonely—thus, unlucky—but a pair of them—a couple—brings happiness.

Love is finite: 'Love is a zero-sum game.' This is perhaps the one I roll my eyes at the most. It assumes that there is a particular finite pot in your heart that has a specific quantity of love in it—like a fixed number of roshogollas. As you give them away to people, they start decreasing in the pot and finally get over. If you give them to many people, each person will have a smaller number of roshogollas. This sense of finiteness is perhaps one of the reasons why people end one relationship to move to another in what is called 'one love at a time'—a kind of sequential monoamory. They like to believe that by ending one, they stop giving love to that person and start serving it to the next. A lesson in thriftiness. I remember my Ma asking me, in a deeply concerned way, a few weeks after I had shared with her my polyamorous life, 'Do you break your heart into tiny pieces and keep giving till it is over, or do you take a little back once in a while so it does not finish quite so soon?' I was both touched by her care and worried about her distress. I remember responding to her with a story she knew well since she is good with Hindu mythology. 'It is like the akshay patra that Krishna gave Draupadi, Ma—to serve unlimited food every day,' I told her quite seriously, hoping she would understand. 'Love is infinite and the heart feels like a bottomless pit.' To me, it is quite dangerous to imagine that if we are being very indiscriminate or extravagant about sharing love, it may one day suddenly finish, leaving us desolate.

Unconventional is unnatural: This belief has two problems. The first is in thinking that conventions are 'natural'. They are not. They are ways of doing things that are constructed over time— often for specific purposes by those who have vested interests in perpetuating certain structures. Bypassing, challenging, breaking, or ignoring them is unconventional, not unnatural. Also, when I hear that statement, I think, how arrogant it is to believe that we already know everything there is to know about the natural world and call something 'unnatural', sealing the possibility of nature throwing surprises at us! We have overestimated the boundaries of our knowledge. The second problem with this belief lies with the valorization of the 'natural' in this context. We wear clothes, we cook food, we attempt to control emotions that may be damaging—these are totally 'unnatural' and have more to do with our development of taste and the choices we make. It is a pity that when it comes to relationships or sex, the 'natural' is invoked as an excuse relentlessly.

Polyamorous people shatter most of these beliefs. They break so many rules of the monoamorous world that, at times, they are feared by society. This fear is born out of both ignorance and discomfort. It is felt, as is the case with any group of rebels who do not stick to the predominant terms of society, that polyamorous people will ruin the current family system and its safety nets that are built on the assumed trust and fidelity in monoamory and by extension, monogamy. But these safety nets that are supposed to keep people secure in their conventional marriages and family structure are worn and riddled with gaping holes through which fall many people and their dreams of a joyful life. Some people also worry that polyamorous people will distract and seduce their spouses who are otherwise tightly fastened with monogamous strings to the sacred marital bed. But the fact that this life is already rife with secret affairs and hidden sexualities is not discussed at all.

While all this apprehension leads to misconceptions about polyamorous people, there is also misinformation actively spread about us. On good days, I am generous and imagine these as acts of self-preservation by the monoamorous society in trepidation of the unknown, wild side of their nature. But on bad days, I see them as malicious slander by people who are so despondent in their own choices that they gain some perverse pleasure out of maligning others. As in every other sphere of life, patriarchy plays a huge role in how these misconceptions play out. Women and other gender and sexual minorities always pay a higher price, and carry the heavier burden of the naming and shaming.

MISCONCEPTIONS ABOUT POLYAMORY

Promiscuous: Indiscriminate, casual, too many transient sexual relationships—the dictionary defines promiscuity in many ways and that's what people attribute to us. In the same way that society imagines sex workers will have sex with anyone for money, without paying any heed to their consent, polyamorous people are also seen as those who must be having sex with everyone. Men often slide into my social inboxes with perverse requests and photos. Without any judgement on people who do like having sex casually and indiscriminately with many people, to assume that a polyamorous person will have sexual relationships with everyone takes away their agency. The same holds true for love. I have to regularly explain to men—even those reputed for their intelligence in the various worlds of arts, academics, or who are otherwise accomplished—who offer love or in the least a kiss, as soon as they get to know I am polyamorous, that I do not feel 'love' towards them. Most often they are surprised, and sometimes they sulk.

Predatory: Since it is believed that we will have sex with everyone around us, we must also be predatory. There is a deep fear that we will somehow thrust ourselves upon innocent bystanders. I know well the suspicious glances I sometimes get from people when I am speaking to their spouses or partners—and especially if I am laughing a lot. It is not a good feeling but it is something we learn to live with. Much like a gay friend had once told me, 'Why do all hetero men feel we are propositioning them—they don't even groom well!' I might apologize for my friend's elitism about grooming, but I don't chide him for his exasperation. I have come to understand over time that this suspicion comes from the insecurity that lies in relationships that struggle with ideas of freedom. Once I started thinking of this with some compassion, I found it easier to cope.

Desperate: Once, when a partner's cousin found out that I was polyamorous, he asked, 'Isn't that attention-seeking?' Many people believe that we are polyamorous because we have failed to find the one true love and in our craving for some sex and affection, we engage with many people. This feels like saying a person is lesbian because she has not found a man! It is ridiculous.

Amoral: Moralities built over generations of conservative thoughts about love, sex, marriage, and family have led to polyamorous people being seen as amoral. Since much of morality is framed through religion, and most religions do not entertain ideas outside of monogamy, polyamory is seen as sinful. As explained in the previous chapter, this has much to do with the emergence of monotheistic Christianity and the idea of being faithful to one god. With this singularity being considered sacred, concepts of poly or multiplicity became profane.

Easy and cheap: There are three problems with polyamorous people being seen as easy and cheap. Firstly, many of us are not. We require copious amounts of work and can be quite lavish in our expectations of time, effort, and money if we want to be—just like anyone else. Secondly, those of us who are easy and cheap believe there is no extra honour or virtue in being difficult and expensive. We feel these are just game-playing tactics to act hard to get and build inaccessibility. If one must play games, we reckon there are more exciting ones. Thirdly and most importantly, parameters such as easy and difficult, cheap and costly, make the whole relationship issue seem like a transactional commodity in a marketplace, where the rules of demand and supply must follow the scarcity principle. According to this principle, the price of a good, which has low supply and high demand, rises to meet the expected demand. Marketers often use the principle to create artificial scarcity and make it exclusive in order to generate a higher demand for it. In the case of relationships, this would mean that if one is difficult (like scarce), then that person will seem very choosy and exclusive and this will create a higher demand for that person. And if someone is easy (like available), that will automatically lower their relative price and demand. It must be so unfortunate to live in a world where rules of economics are mirrored in love.

Pathological: Sex addict, nymphomaniac, pervert, sex fiend—you take your pick. Some people feel being polyamorous is a disease. I am reminded of the days when queer people would be sent to get 'fixed'. In some parts of the world, they still suffer the 'conversion' treatments. Similarly, polyamorous people are pathologized and treated like they are suffering a mental illness that makes them the way they are. After I had given a talk to a well-educated and liberal audience, a woman came up to me and asked if I have ever tried to 'cure' myself. She looked at my flabbergasted expression and added that she was telling me this for my own good so I could have a normal life! Yet again I realized that there is nothing scarier than people with 'good intentions'.

Shallow and short-term: Many people feel that our relationships are shallow. Plurality is translated as superficial and trivial. The assumption negates the capacity of the human heart to be able to do more. However, no one will tell a person with many siblings that it is not possible for them to love them all deeply. Another misconception about us is that we do not have the desire, intent, or ability to build deep and long-term relationships. They think we have no concept of loyalty to partners, no fidelity in our relationship with them, and are afraid of commitment. They believe that we are only motivated by our need to satisfy our desires. Shirking the responsibilities that otherwise come with one steady relationship, we flit across many. Any polyamorous person will tell you that this is not true. I agree that it is difficult to imagine concepts like loyalty, commitment, care, and responsibility outside the framework of two individuals and positioning them in a world where multiple relationships coexist. But similar redefinitions have been made earlier across borders of gender and sexualities too. We especially have much to learn from our queer elders. For us, loyalty, commitment, and fidelity are defined more by what we feel for each other, rather than what we are barred from doing with others. For us, care and responsibility include a larger sphere of people connected to us through our partners—their other partners and extended families. Much like families in the monoamorous world that are made with interconnections of people related by birth and marriage, in our world, these families are created through relationships of affection and trust. It is time we consider these as equally valid foundations for building families.

It is all about sex: This is perhaps at the heart of all the other misconceptions. Society feels that being polyamorous is only about having sex with multiple people. In reality, many polyamorous people I know are asexual or while being sexual, do not consider it the most important aspect of romantic relationships. Unfortunately, a predominantly heteronormative world has conflated love and sex to the extent that it has become impossible to think of one without the other. For me and many others, at the heart of being polyamorous lie the desire, ability, practice, and struggle of loving more than one person concurrently, with or without sexual intimacies. Needless to say, making it all about sex takes away from polyamory the core emotional and spirited connections that are built and nurtured.

These misconceptions are unfortunate. Not only do they create wrong impressions about who we are and why we love the way we do, but they also make our lives seem unabashedly decadent without any sense of struggle, hurt, or questions. They make us feel so much less than who we are, but at the same time so glamorized! That is the other problem of this kind of stereotyping. In comparison to our supposedly free and wanton lives, those of monoamorous people seem insipid and uninspiring. Without the difficulties of our lives being out there, their lives seem the only ones riddled with problems and burdens. If we did make an honest evaluation of both our lives, we would see that we have more in common than we think. We will understand that in love and life, there is only hope and no guarantees—no matter how many people we are in love with. We would then be able to share our heartaches and either weep together, or croon, 'Jab pyar kiya to darna kya? (When one has loved, what is the fear?)' à la Lata Mangeshkar in *Mughal-E-Azam* (1960).

OFFERING KINDNESS

However, while these allegations can be hard to live with, it is important for us to keep talking about polyamory, engaging, expressing, and explaining. This generation of polyamorous people has come together in solidarity and support groups, and we are slowly finding our language and struggling to create a space for ourselves in society. While that helps us to live, stay safe, and cope with the discriminations we face, it is also the responsibility of our generation to begin conversations about us with the rest of the world.

Let me give an example from another world, which I was entering hesitantly. I will never forget what my dear friend Rumi Harish did for me then. I was new to understanding the world of transgender people. I was frequently making mistakes of dead-naming them, introducing them incorrectly, and making stupid mistakes with their pronouns. This was making me nervous, guilty, and shy. Rumi corrected me many times with affection and patience. He told me that it was alright to make mistakes as long as I knew it and rectified myself. He, a trans man, poet, musician, activist, and artist, whom I had known in his past life as a different person, eased my entry into his world with gentle handholding and great kindness. I hope we, as polyamorous people, can also offer this kindness to those who have been making an effort to understand and reach out to us. Because, of late, I have come to realize that much of the misconceptions that people have about us come from anxiety and insecurities in their own lives.

WHO WANTS TO BE FREE?

Finally, let me present a different thought I have recently had. A monoamorous friend told me, 'Nobody is actually mono, Aru. We are all having affairs, flings, switching partners, and sleeping around. We just do it in secret, quietly, without rocking the boat. Everyone knows, everyone denies, and everyone plays into the conspiracy of silence. And come to think of it, isn't it more pleasurable that way—the risk of getting caught makes it so much more thrilling, doesn't it?' When I think of polyamory being perhaps the last taboo in our society, I also think of the idea of the forbidden, and thus the enchantment it might have for people. The forbidden draws people to its secret delicious heart and the shame, fear, and guilt of committing such a transgression becomes the core of its pleasure. Are polyamorous people painted sinful so that this kind of love remains illicit? Are we kept outside the margins of what is acceptable, so we can continuously offer the promise of hidden, scandalous delight—much like tawaifs and courtesans?

Before I could make up my mind, something else happened. A friend came to me quite agitated. He said that after reading an article I had written on polyamory for a newspaper, his partner told him about her relationship with another man that was counting its third year. She told him she needed to be honest with him. She loved them both, and wasn't going to choose. He told me he didn't care about honesty at all. He didn't need to know. Everything was fine as it was. 'But doesn't it make you feel free of lies, deception?' I asked, hopefully. 'Who wants to be free!' he said in a state of grave agitation. He may not, but this freedom, I realized, remains of deep significance to polyamorous people. And they live through their struggles against all these misconceptions because of it.

3

A THOUSAND LOVES SUCH AS THESE: WAYS OF BEING POLYAMOROUS

In my late teens, when the butterflies in my heart started fluttering with what I realized was the desperate need to fall in love like every silver-screen heroine I had witnessed till then, there were a million songs from Bangla and Hindi films available to express my longing. From 'Yaad aa rahi hai (I am remembering you)' of *Love Story* (1981), 'Gazab ka hai din socho zara (Just think how amazing these days are)' from *Qayamat Se Qayamat Tak* (1988), to 'Dil deewana bin sajna ke maane na (Without a lover I cannot control this mad heart)' from *Maine Pyar Kiya* (1989)—the hit numbers were all about love—love longed for, love found, love lost. Films, the main source of entertainment and sanctuary for imagination those days, revolved around love, as did our slow, post-school afternoons of giggling friends whispering about the goings-on between girls and boys we knew. In all of this our vital takeaways were two important things: 1) Life was useless unless you found love, and 2) Love was pointless unless it was the 'one true love'. And we all acquired the anxiety of being declared useless and pointless if we failed.

But I had different emotions that led to other kinds of failures. I would fall in love with more than one person at the same time. While I felt disoriented in a very monoamorous universe around me, there was, deep inside me, a voice that told me this wasn't wrong, that this too had a place in the world. But I had neither the courage to speak up, nor the language to express any of this. Nothing around me in art, literature, or songs came close to relating what I felt. I found out much later that this desolation that I experienced in those early days is shared by many polyamorous people. A friend erupted, 'I felt angry, I felt lonely, I felt stupid, and I felt I was a bad person—it was too much to carry, so much easier to just give in.'

When in my early twenties, I first heard Ghalib's 'Hazaron Khwahishein Aisi' in Jagjit Singh's rendition for the TV serial *Ghalib,* I was astounded! The lyrics went:

Hazaron khwahishein aisi ki har khvahish pe dam nikle
Bahut nikle mere arman lekin phir bhi kam nikle

(A thousand desires such as these, each worth dying for So many of them have been expressed, yet there are more to come)

I still remember the profound impact these words had on me. Something rested at the pit of my stomach. I finally felt understood. Each of my loves was just as strong and deep as the other. And all of them true. Just like the poet said. These words, since then, have been at the heart of my practice of polyamory.

BURDEN OF DEFINITIONS

There are as many ways of defining polyamory as there are polyamorous people. For me, it has meant the desire, ability, and practice of loving more than one person at a time, with the intention of forming nurturing and enduring relationships, with the consent of all involved. These could be with or without physical or sexual intimacies, but always with an emotional connection that involves caring for and remaining invested in the other person's well-being. However, there are some polyamorous folks who define polyamory as relationships where there is both love and sexual desire; others who do not engage in deep emotional relationships with more than one person while keeping their sexual and other intimacies plural; and still others who consider any relationship, long or short, deep or not, emotional or sexual, as part of their explorations in polyamory. There are many asexual people engaged in polyamory too. For me, the emotional, intellectual, and political connects are a must. It has become more so over the past few years, with the growing threat of strong Hindutva right-wing forces polarizing our already fragmented worlds in India.

What has been most important for me about being polyamorous is that I can love to my heart's content. Sometimes I hear people refer to polyamory as just 'poly'. That means 'many', I say; 'Where is the "love"?' I ask. When my friends sound worried about my way of loving, I give them the example of the Kalpataru tree, a wish-fulfilling, eternally giving tree in Hindu mythology. The heart is capable of loving infinitely. To surrender its definition to a zero-sum game is accepting failure in the face of a conspiracy part patriarchal and part capitalistic.

Often people wonder about the durability of polyamorous relationships. Most assume these are quickies—short bursts of great sex and if lucky, some romance too. Reality is quite different and varied. Talking about the durability of relationships, however, always feels like one is discussing the shelf-life of products. In monoamory and monogamy, one enters into a relationship with the hope of 'till death do us part'. Even the very cynical ones, who may realize the fallacy of this, continue to play along. But in polyamory, one does not necessarily have duration in mind when starting a relationship. 'How this will work out' is more of a concern than 'how long this will last'—making quality more of a consideration than longevity. So here, relationships can be short- or long-term, some fleeting even after promises of more, others starting off as 'let's see' and growing into long-standing wonders! Many relationships shift, change, and transform over time due to distance or life-changing circumstances. However, for me, unless abused or exploited, if there is some break in a relationship, I consider it a semicolon and not a full-stop. This means that I cannot stop loving someone once I have begun to love them. While the nature and texture of the relationships may change, including the levels of intimacies, at the heart of it remains a deep sense of love and commitment.

Another question that comes up often is the number of partners one must have before qualifying as 'polyamorous'. Thankfully, unlike the list of Indian billionaires in the Fortune 500, being certified as polyamorous does not require a specific number of acquisitions of partners. You are polyamorous if you believe in the concept and think you are. As a polyamorous person, one may even be single—out of choice, necessity, or limitations; or have just one partner for the time being while being fully aware of other possibilities; or have more than one partner. The image of a polyamorous person with a calendar chock-a-block with partner-dates is only wishful thinking. Also, anyone who has been in a relationship worth talking about knows the kind of time and energy it takes. In polyamory, imagine multiplying that by the number of relationships one has. It makes it very hard for those of us who lead otherwise busy lives to pursue so many relationships. So, the numbers really don't matter that much. The crux of this kind of living is to always know that the body and heart are free to fall in love if and when they want to, in an environment of honesty and consent.

However, one must remember that once the restrictions of monoamory and heteronormative lives are lifted, there are myriad possibilities of being that emerge. Only some of these can be termed polyamorous. Strict and fixed definitions of either polyamory or this larger universe of non-mono non-hetero lives tend to kill the very purpose of fluidity, tentativeness, and exploration that is at the heart of this breaking away from convention. This is about giving ourselves the permission to walk the wilderness of spirit deeply embedded and waiting inside most of us. A friend recently told me, 'To be polyamorous is to have the freedom to be what I still can't imagine.' I would say that it also gives me the pleasure to define what chains my freedom will engage with.

SPECTRUM OF PRACTICES

Books on polyamory published in the Western world have a long list of various structures of polyamory that are practised there. From 'parallel' to 'kitchen table' to 'garden party', there are different names for the spectrum of practices that have evolved over time. This spectrum of practices is mostly classified around two key parameters: the prioritization of partners depending on the extent of intimacy—physical, sexual, or emotional; and the relationships between the various partners of polyamorous people who are connected to each other through the common loved one.

As far as prioritization of partners goes, many polyamorous people have a primary partner whom they place at the centre of their life. All their other relationships are secondary to this one. The primary partner may or may not be living with them or married to them. If they do live together, then they are called nesting partners. Often, the primary partner has more power than other partners in setting rules and boundaries for their relationships. This hierarchy is reflected in the way the other relationships must accommodate this one. However, primary partnerships can shift and change through time like any relationship. One important warning here is that given the powers they enjoy, primary partners have to be alert not to fall back on the conditioning of monoamory in the restrictions they impose on their relationships.

There are polyamorous people who don't have primary partners. It could be because they believe in non-hierarchical relationships or that they have not yet found anyone to be primary partners with. Here, all partners enjoy more or less equal space, intensity, and powers. This happens even if some of them may be sharing domesticities, or living in the same city, while others are farther away.

There are also those who are polyamorous but prefer to lead a solo life, away from their various partners. They do not share domesticity and everything it encompasses with any one partner. They may have a primary partner, or multiple primary partners, or none at all. Some may even be single and not have any partner at any point of time. This kind of solo polyamory is what I strongly identify with and thus have dedicated a whole chapter later to explore the contours of how that works out for some of us.

Sometimes, polyamorous people may have multiple primary partners, and other partners. In theory, the living scenario can be quite varied for such people. There are those who share time across multiple households; those who live with one primary partner but ensure enough time and space with the others; and those who just prefer to live alone, equidistant from all their primary partners. However, in practical terms, I have seen people struggle with this a lot, especially when the strain and demands of managing multiple primary relationships starts endangering other relationships. Sometimes, we still carry vestiges of monoamory in us and the poly situation works as long as we know we are primary at least in someone's life! It becomes easier to experiment with loyalty and fidelity and control jealousy when there is one place where we know we come first. The hierarchy of the 'only one' of monoamory starts to morph a little and emerge as the 'first on the list' in this case. This confidence and the ability to remain open start to crack sometimes, when multiple primaries emerge in our partner's life. From the stories I have heard, this has been the cause of some polyamorous break-ups!

Moreover, while there is hierarchy that is created with intention and acceptance among partners, there is also 'hierarchy of experience', where a partner may feel a sense of being low-priority due to a situation or actions by their loved one even without their partner intending to build any sense of hierarchy. Often, the accused partner tries to rationalize their behaviour, which is quite useless in this situation. It can be more hurtful to deny someone their experiential truth. Therefore, in such cases, open conversations may help resolve unequal expectations among them.

There is one group of people in this spectrum who still provoke debates even within polyamorous circles. They are people who believe in 'relationship anarchy'. Here, a person spontaneously and independently engages in various partnerships without the responsibilities towards one limiting the engagements with another. Many such folks do not distinguish between a partner and a non-partner, which can create difficulties in understanding them. Sometimes, they are seen with suspicion even among polyamorous circles, much like what bisexual or pansexual folks sometimes face within queer worlds. This is an example of how, even among people who defy the boundaries of convention to create radical relationship frameworks, there is tension at the margins about how far one can go!

Practices also differ in how a set of polyamorous people connected through one partner relate to each other. In some cases, they don't, and prefer to remain in parallel worlds. In other cases, they may choose to know each other, while deciding how close they want to be. There are also times when polyamorous people create an alternative circle of family with their various partners and co-lovers. These may be rare or not so much 'out there' yet in the Indian context, but I have met a few and find it quite an amazing, albeit challenging, way to live in love and friendship. They may not all always live together but are there for each other just like a family. Much like the chosen families of queer folks, these families show us that it is possible to build new ways of living that are collaborative, empathetic, and less lonely in a world where conventional marriages and families are imploding all around us.

What one defines as and how one practises polyamory have an impact on not just the self, but also on partners, their partners, children, and other family members connected to us. These determine power dynamics, how needs and expectations are both expressed and met, means of framing rules and boundaries, and ways in which conflicts arising out of these relationships are resolved. They also influence the ways in which a polyamorous person dates and looks out for new relationships, or how they decide to end relationships. Since the spectrum of practices is very wide and diverse, it is important to understand them to comprehend and engage with polyamorous people. Those who are thinking of engaging in this way of being will have to figure out the best possible practices that work for them.

POLYAMORY, WITH CHILDREN

In most parts of the world, even today, parenting is a right enjoyed only by heteronormative monogamous married folks. If you are queer or single, you are seen as deviant. Even if tolerable within the limits of law in some countries, you are certainly not considered eligible, capable, or deserving of bringing up children. Polyamorous folks suffer the same stigma even in countries where they have been open and out for a while now. In India, I have not met too many people who openly live with children in polyamorous families, but I have witnessed a few engaged in co-parenting, with a foundation of love, friendship, and trust. However, polyamorous families where multiple adults take responsibilities for children are seen with much suspicion. Just like gay men who have been the victims of the prejudice that they are paedophiles, adults in a polyamorous family are doubted as bearing sinister motives.

However, members of most polyamorous families who bring up children collectively have repeatedly mentioned how much easier and less strenuous it is for them to share the work and roles of raising kids in a 'tribe'—their chosen family. They talk about the comfort of knowing that from very early years, their children interact deeply with different people as parents, who have diverse perspectives on life, and can be role models for a variety of aspirations. They also emphasize the importance of explaining to children the nature of polyamorous families as these are different from the conventional monogamous, heteronormative families they will interact with in their places of education and society at large. On the question of whether children may be affected adversely by differences among the caregivers, as it may happen in the case of polyamorous families, it is rather believed that children who grow up in this 'different' kind of environment imbibe the capacity to understand, adapt to, and thrive when there are changes in their surroundings—skills that adults often pay a huge amount of time and money to acquire later in life.

THE INDIAN CONTEXT

One of the reasons for writing this book was my difficulty in connecting with some of the wonderful yet alien material that was coming my way through books written in the West. While many of the joys and hurdles of practising polyamory in our country are the same as theirs, there are many differences in the social environments. The polyamorous people whom I have met in India have to struggle with very specific issues of the Indian context. This starts with the very idea of what it means to have the 'freedom to choose' a particular kind of life here.

To begin with, the amount of control and impact families have on our lives is much higher and more complex in India. Most of us never quite 'leave home' unless forced to. Families often remain central in much of our decision-making, including romantic and financial. With families also comes care for the elderly, which is seen, in India, as the responsibility of the next generation. While this may be changing slowly, most of us still hold on to the values of looking after the elderly in our homes. Indian homes are busy, crowded spaces. Many homes are still places where multiple nuclear families live, with many siblings, parents, grandparents, and sometimes an odd mix of other extended family members. This makes personal choices about domesticities and domestic space that much more complicated. Marriages are seen as absolutely necessary institutions that hold together the family and thereby the societal structure, while divorces are frowned upon. Even with more and more people choosing to not marry or to simply live together in some urban areas, the larger part of the country still sees these as aberrations at best, and at worst, sinful.

In most of India, social practices and prejudices determine how differences in gender and sexuality are perceived. They affect different genders differently, even on dating and matrimonial sites. There is still severe stigma attached to being queer in most parts of Indian society. Religion and caste have always played major roles in marriages and kinship in India. The tradition of 'arranged marriage' in the country is conducted strictly within caste, class, and religious boundaries. But often, even those who choose their partners outside of this convention, function out of deeply entrenched biases to auto-select people within their social spheres of homogenous religion, caste, and class positions. Women, Dalits, and people of sexual minorities still face immense violence and are judged severely when they transgress boundaries. With 'honour killings' and 'anti-Romeo squads', who one partners with and how one's desire manifests is dangerous territory, and a searing political question in India.

All of these factors impact polyamorous lives and how we practise polyamory in India, making it different from how it manifests in other countries. The very exploration of such a life choice is severely restricted, as is dating, or the thought of coming out as polyamorous people leading open lives. Often, in India, to love is to put one's life at risk.

SAFE SEX

A significant aspect of polyamory is to understand the health risks attached to having multiple partners and the possibilities of transmitting sexual diseases. Thus, practising safety during sex is of primary importance. Other than using various kinds of barriers during sex, testing oneself regularly becomes necessary as one engages sexually with more people. It is also important to seek testing information of partners and decide for oneself how much risk one would be willing to take. Since, in polyamorous lives, our connections are with more than one person, our safe sex responsibilities also extend to more than our own partners. There are those within a polyamorous framework who abide by the concept of 'fluid fidelity', where they limit the exchange of bodily fluids just amongst themselves or within known and trusted circles. Balancing desire and risk becomes crucial in most relationships.

However, most polyamorous people also feel that there is more safety in these relationships than in monoamorous ones. Here, the fact that one may have more than one sexual partner is open and understood. Requesting to be tested or using safe sex methods in no way casts any aspersions on partners and are dealt with as regular and natural behaviour. However, in the monoamorous world, where the basic foundation of relationships lies on the fact that there is fidelity with only one partner, this becomes a problem. The assumption of fidelity is often incorrect since secret affairs and flings go on aplenty there. But ensuring safe sex with testing becomes hard. 'My husband takes huge umbrage to suggestions of safety or testing,' a monoamorous friend had told me. 'He thinks I suspect him of sleeping around!' she added. Since monoamorous people hold on to the idea of having a single partner as a moral issue, any suggestion for testing or safe sex to protect oneself is seen as an insult, suspecting their moral fibre.

WORK IN PROGRESS

Polyamorous living is a dynamic process, a continuous work in progress. One could say that any relationship should be that way since we learn, grow, and change with time and experiences in life. But in polyamory, this becomes more important because of two reasons. Firstly, the intricate threads of relationships are delicately held together by more than two people who are interconnected through their partners, and changes in any one of their lives and choices have the possibility of impacting others in the network. Secondly, before any such changes are implemented, they would need to be agreed upon, or at least negotiated with more than two people. Since, often, we do not find answers to our questions or solutions to conflicts in precedence set by monoamorous worlds, we have to improvise and resolve them ourselves. In the process, the world is never quite settled and final for us.

There is also the debate over the definitions of a 'lover' and a 'partner' in polyamory, and when one becomes the other. For most polyamorous people, 'lover' is a term for someone at the beginning of a relationship, where it is still unclear where this might go, whereas 'partner' is a term for someone in a more established form of relationship that happens over time and with mutual agreement. In this book, I have used the terms specifically where the difference in their definition is important to the discussion, and interchangeably where the difference does not matter in the topic being discussed. These loose definitions and openness are also significant aspects of polyamory, providing easy navigation between the two. Some polyamorous people also like to remain fluid and queer about their relative positions on sexuality and gender in relationships. There are experiments that are practised actively to interrogate, challenge, or break various rules of relationships. These 'becomings' are in continuous motion and shift gears as and when new experiences or insights emerge. Some of us argue that much like being queer, being polyamorous is both a way of living and a state of mind.

ONE LOVE AT A TIME

There are many people who see themselves as monoamorous— loving only one person at a time—but say they are open to having one such relationship after another. They qualify their monoamory with this 'one love at a time' concept. I find this qualifier difficult to understand. In monoamory, one gets into a relationship in good faith and hopes for it to last. Sometimes it does, and sometimes it does not. If it ends, one grieves and tries to move on. Life willing, one finds another person to love and be loved by. And this continues. So, what is the need to add this qualifier specifically? Surely it isn't about keeping score? Or does it mean that one sees every relationship as temporary, with a finite and limited shelf-life? Or that the only way one knows to move forward, if one falls in love once more, is to end one relationship to enter another?

To me, adding this qualifier of sequential love to their identity as a monoamorous person reveals a deep-seated anxiety about being judged in case their relationships don't work, and they cannot hold on to the super glorified 'one true' forever. Adding the qualifier distances them from being in the radar of that judgement, and yet protects them from falling into the unknown and uneasy ambit of polyamory. A bit of fence-sitting, this. In some cases, the qualifier may also be used as a buffer for those whose emotional need for the apparent security of monoamory contradicts both their intellectual critique of it as well as genuine curiosity about polyamory. So, this cushion of space between monoamory and polyamory gives them relative comfort.

When faced with more than one possibility of relationship, deciding to end one love in whatever state it is in, to live with the other without really exploring any other possibility, is severely life-limiting. Often, attachments, emotions, desires, and expectations linger in various forms and textures with the love that is terminated or severely curtailed. This, in my experience, weighs down the relationship that is chosen to continue. The contours of both remain blurred while the self keeps going back and forth. In the process, there is not just heartache for those involved, but resentment builds towards both relationships—neither of which has allowed the full potential of the other to flourish. This does not have to be so brutal and unforgiving if one allows oneself the permission to think in polyamorous ways.

WHY BE POLYAMOROUS

Finally, the question that lingers on—why all this trouble to be polyamorous? And then, more questions tumble out—is one born this way? Is it a choice? Is it an identity? A lifestyle?

I collated many responses to these questions from the various conversations I have had over the years. Some of us feel we are polyamorous because this relieves us from the pressure to be the only person fulfilling all their partner's needs and desires. This burden of being the 'one' in this glorified land of 'two' often leads to people feeling inadequate and miserable. Polyamory releases us from making that same demand of our partners. Some of us feel that intimacy with different people gives us different perspectives in life. It allows us to keep our minds open as much as our hearts, so as to develop close bonds with people with a spectrum of ways of thinking about life.

For me, a very important aspect of being polyamorous has been to discover the different 'people' that inhabit me, who are invited out into the open by the different people I love. It is like sitting in a room surrounded by mirrors that reflect me from various angles. I am often surprised to see how my interactions and the texture of relationships are so different with different partners. I play distinctly diverse roles in their lives too. This discovery of the many 'me', as shared by other polyamorous friends, reminds me so much of the song Zahid Ahmed, adoringly called 'pagla' or 'mad' Zahid in Bangladesh, had written in Bangla:

Tomar ghore bash kore kara o mon jano na, tomar
ghore boshot kore koi jona
Ek jone shur tole ektare o mon, arek jone mandirate tal
tole, o mon
Abar beshura shur dhore dyakho kon jona, kon jona
Tomar ghore boshot kore koi jona, o mon jano na
Tomar ghore boshot kore koi jona

(Who are the people residing in your home, o heart you
don't know, how many people live in your home—
One plucks a tune on the ektara, o heart, and another
picks a beat on the mandira
And see, yet another, hums a tuneless tune, who is that,
who is that?
How many people live in your home, o heart you don't
know—
How many people live in your home)

[Ektara: Single-stringed instrument
Mandira: Small, bell-shaped cymbals]

Many people I spoke to have lived monoamorous lives before
accepting polyamory. The choice of polyamory gave them a more
truthful alternative to live by. Here, the meanings of freedom and
responsibility are co-created by different partners instead of being
handed down as legacy. To many of us, the idea of being able
to shape our relationships along mutually agreeable boundaries
without the fear of being judged is an important reason for being
polyamorous. A cheeky one told me, 'It's so that I never wonder
what could have been, Aru, and die in regret.'

There is a case to be made for those among us who are bisexual
or pansexual. Monoamory, for them, would mean shutting off
a part of their universe of desire, no matter what the gender of
their partner is. For them, being polyamorous is the only way to
express themselves fully. Some of us feel we are born this way,
and some have chosen this as a way of being—that does not
really matter. What matters is how we live this life—with honesty
and compassion.

I am polyamorous because my heart sees beauty, courage, kindness, and compassion in more than one person and desires to connect with them. The same reasons for which anyone would fall in love with one person, I fall for more than one person. I just refuse to say, 'Stop. Your quota is done.'

What John Berger wrote in G (1972) rings true for me at many levels: 'Never again will a single story be told as though it were the only one.' Society's absolute obsession with 'one'—'one love', 'one goal', and 'one life'—suffocates me. Its fierce focus is energy-depleting, its sense of arrogance shocking. The idea that 'more than one is better than one' is perhaps connected to my faith in diversity, in the collective, and in our ability to process the 'many' in our lives.

As I witness in the political arena of India—this land of diverse civilizations—a huge strategic plan in motion to create 'one nation, one culture' that feeds into the logic of 'one leader', I realize my distaste for 'one' may have stronger roots. I now feel that polyamory is an extension of a deeper political belief, where I trust in a polyphonic universe where one listens to many different songs flowing down many rivers.

4

BOAT OF HOPE I
'HONESTY HAS BURDENS TOO, THAT OTHER PEOPLE HAVE TO BEAR'

Sidharth Sarcar is a landscape architect and works as a freelance consultant. He is in his early thirties. Mandeep Raikhy is a contemporary dancer, choreographer, and dance scholar. He is in his early forties. Both use he/him as their pronouns. They have been in a relationship for eight years now. Over the past two years, they have shared domestic space as primary partners, living together in Delhi. They started their relationship being open and honest to each other about other sexual encounters. Over time, they have begun learning about and exploring polyamory at their own pace. I had the privilege of a conversation with them on how they feel, think, and practise the idea of sex and romance with more than one partner. Here are excerpts from our conversation.

(A. G.: Arundhati Ghosh / S. S.: Sidharth Sarcar / M. R.: Mandeep Raikhy)

ON DISCOVERING POLYAMORY

A. G.: How did you come across the idea of polyamory?

S. S.: I think even the idea of having an open relationship from a sexual point of view is something that came to me because of restraint. I was struggling to be physically content with just one person. The emotional attachment was strong, but the physical needs were different. And I was cheating. So when I met Mandeep, who was also coming out of a situation where he too had thought about opening up to many possibilities, we decided to keep an open relationship sexually. We both agreed on a set of loosely formed rules. Then, at some point, a few years later, I encountered the idea of polyamory when I met someone interesting and wanted to extend it beyond physicality. I realized I was holding myself back because of the relationship I had with Mandeep. At that point, Mandeep and I started talking seriously about aspects of other relationships beyond sex. We started discussing polyamory.

M. R.: I experienced the need for it in someone else first. Before Sidharth, I was in a relationship with a polyamorous person. He asked me if he could continue to have his other relationships. But I was coming into this after thirteen years of no relationships, and was not ready for it at all. For me, it had to be completely monoamorous. And I forced him to do something that he wasn't really cut out for. But those two years, I constantly felt insecure because things would be brewing, hidden from me, and I could feel it. That had to end. Then I met Sidharth. By then, I had realized that if I was so insecure even in a relationship where we were not supposed to have sex with anyone else, then the strength of a relationship had to be not so much about the other people but more about trust, honesty, and communication between us. I was happy to try out with Sidharth something that I hadn't done before or even imagined doing. We began our relationship with the rule that we would have open sexual relationships and if we felt something was more than just a sexual encounter, then we would bring it to the table and discuss it. Yes, we did make a transition from open sexual relationships to actually talking about polyamory.

ON DIFFERENCES IN PRACTICE

A. G.: Is your practice of polyamory similar to each other's?

M. R.: So, my understanding of polyamory is probably similar to his. But in practice, it is different—at least, it has been different so far. I have sexual encounters with people but there's not enough room in my life, at least so I think, to bring in another relationship right now. I feel like it's so much labour. I don't have the time and the bandwidth for that labour, for a full playout. Falling in love, for me, is somehow a deliberate activity. You make space for it, and then it happens. Not otherwise. In my twenties, it was different. I would fall in love more regularly. Earlier, in my teenage years, I would fall in love left right and centre. But at this point in my life, I have learnt to do some 'border-control' in love. I must say I have developed very good immunity to any kind of encounter or potential relationship that can be one-sided or toxic. Very different from my twenties and thirties, where I would chase men offering such equations. But once I realized and worked on the fact that it had everything to do with my relationship with my father, I started to recognize and stop it. So, this border-control has to do with me and my mind space and almost nothing to do with Sidharth or my relationship with him.

A. G.: *Do you not fall in love with anyone at all?*

M. R.: In fact, I recently encountered somebody for whom, after a long time, I said to myself, 'Oh, it could be something more than a sexual encounter.' But, through a few interactions, I realized that this was potentially one of those things where, if I allowed myself to fall into it, it would feel like an unequal relationship. Like I had to chase it. I felt I had to wait for two days for a text message. I pulled back. But if I allowed it, it could become another relationship. We're in touch but he has not entered the inner space.

A. G.: *And what about you, Sidharth?*

M. R.: He has an open heart. All his windows are open. I understood this need in him very early on—that he would want to go beyond sexual encounters. And right now, he does have another person in his life.

S. S.: I have a lot more time in hand compared to Mandeep and I feel time is a big factor that helps me pursue a relationship. Every time I meet someone, even if it is the smallest feeling beyond sex that appears in my mind and heart, I pursue it. I don't think, 'Oh it is not right,' or 'I am not supposed to be doing this.' So, I think I am intrinsically polyamorous and for a long time, I was shutting out these feelings. But now when I feel it, I go with that feeling. I am extremely honest from the beginning. When I meet someone, they know that Mandeep is there. He is my primary partner. And knowing that helps them decide if they want to proceed or not. These days, if anyone asks me, I say Mandeep is my primary partner but there is another person as well. But Mandeep, in your case too, I think your relationships with the people you have sexual encounters with, especially those you meet regularly—there is a different kind of polyamory there, isn't it? You have feelings too. I think it's not as defined as mine because you probably don't hang out with them. But there is some kind of affection that you have.

M. R.: For sure. Of course, there is no repeated sexual encounter without love. I think there is something there, some exchange that happens.

S. S.: I don't think you have acknowledged it the way I have, in the way I pursue it, like going out on a date, doing dinner together, and all that.

M. R.: Yeah, well, that I don't do.

S. S.: You know, Arundhati, I was very excited about the possibility of Mandeep having a relationship beyond his sexual encounters. I feel like it's more equal and fairer if it's similar for both of us. But I want him to do it at his own pace and I think he will do it when he has more time.

M. R.: I think while in sexual relationships I am certainly poly, whether I can be in love with multiple people at the same time is a question. Theoretically, I know it's possible. But I haven't experienced it, or I should say I haven't practised it yet. Maybe there is lack of time, or a mental block. But I feel like I'm becoming more and more open to the idea.

ON RULES AND HONESTY

A. G.: How honest are you with each other?

M. R.: There is a negotiation on how much detail will be shared. Initially, I didn't want to know anything. And then at some point, I got comfortable with some details. But I like information when I ask for it. When I am ready. There is an unsaid agreement that you share only if I am asking. Otherwise, I get irritated and say that I don't want to know everything.

S. S.: Our comfort in talking about the men in our lives has increased with time. From not sharing anything, to sharing some and what is asked for. I am totally different from Mandeep here. I am curious and want to know everything. I also come from a place where, in my past relationships, I've hidden information and cheated. So, in this relationship, initially, I used to be overly honest—to the point that it made Mandeep mad. I used to share too much in too little time. I used to think I was doing the right thing, that I was being ethical and cleansing myself. I did not realize that this was causing some kind of pain to Mandeep. That was also brought to the table and we discussed it. We have come to an understanding about it now.

M. R.: I think, now, I can take a lot more detail than before. I feel secure. But even now, I don't want to know things too quickly. I need time to absorb them. It is partially to preserve myself, to not be shaken up. But of course, there have been instances where I have been worried about Sidharth's well-being in a relationship and stepped in to tell him. It is when I have sensed that his dynamics with the other person weren't healthy. Sidharth has a history of chasing unavailable men and being in toxic relationships. I have been honest with him if I have seen something like that.

S. S.: And you were spot-on the time you did intervene. I trusted what you told me. But of course, I listened and took the call myself to cut away from that person. Mandeep and I have always had great communication. We talk and discuss a lot. Even when we don't agree. That is also what we have mutually agreed upon for this relationship.

ON TRUST AND SECURITY

A. G.: What does trust mean to you?

S. S.: Trust, for me, is related to the idea of abandonment. Most of my issues around trust come from feeling constantly abandoned as a child. So, I think, is this person really in love with me? Or is it because I'm younger etc.? I'm being honest. In my head, I've always run through Mandeep's earlier partners; I'm definitely a different person. He never agrees though. While I love the arts and we are constantly surrounded by artists, I am an architect with a nine-to-five technical job. I feel I am an outsider to this arts world. I used to worry if I would be abandoned because of that. There are still vestiges of that—even now. But what Mandeep does to make me feel safe and belong, is 'trust' for me. He has always made me feel so secure. He has never abandoned me in front of his parents. We have dealt with all the problems with both our parents together. He has also taken decisions based on my position in his life. At the beginning, for somebody who was ten or eleven years older than me, for him to come and stay with me at hostels—all those things add up. With time, the relationship has gotten so secure. I know this person is not going to walk all over me or let go of me. I am somebody of great importance. Even if I killed someone, he would....

M. R.: Wow.

S. S.: No, no, I am not being dramatic. You would surely send me to jail. But this wouldn't be a reason for you to leave me. I will give another example. I remember the last time somebody wanted to stay back after a sexual encounter with Mandeep at our house; he called and checked with me if it was okay. I found it sweet that he was checking in with me and that he also wanted to know what I was doing. This is trust. We have reached a stage where there are times when he says, 'You know somebody's coming over. Can you come later?' Or I say, 'Hey, I'm going to be late. I'm going to somebody's place.' We have reached that level of comfort. That has also taken time.

M. R.: For me, the trust that has grown over time is actually trust with myself. Within this relationship I began to trust that I am secure enough in myself and my body. I will not be threatened by details of encounters that happen outside of this relationship. If he sleeps with someone who is more beautiful than me or has a better body or is better in some respect, I have learnt to deal with it. Those insecurities can threaten you. Over time, I have built enough security in myself. His encounters and his being with other people are not threatening to me, to my sense of myself. I think this has been quite a nice journey to go through.

A. G.: *What do you think enables this journey?*

M. R.: In the beginning, it was through words he used, like, 'This is my primary relationship.' It meant a lot for me. But you can only really feel settled with it and trust it when you live through it. Now, we're at a point where I know I mean something in this relationship. We had a moment last year when there was another person in the picture for him and he felt it was a little bit more than just a sexual encounter. I was in a really weak place health-wise at that time. I felt like I couldn't digest this. I realized he was guarding me from the details of what was happening, but I knew we had to bring it to the table. And we did. Then he made the decision to shut that down for the moment, for me. I think that gave me trust in him. I felt my needs were being heard, being prioritized. Especially when I was very vulnerable. That matters—the time matters.

S. S.: It was a very important time for us. When we discussed this, he did not give me a deadline or anything. He only told me, very sweetly, that it was starting to bother him a bit. But he said that I should perhaps give us a break. He wasn't asking me to cut off the other relationship. He just needed to fix some things around himself. I thought, as a primary partner and for the place that he had in my heart, I had to make a decision. He was fragile. I knew that. I knew from previous instances that when Mandeep is physically vulnerable, which is not very often, he needs care. So, I took the call to shut the other thing down for the time being. But the person is back in my life now. It happened two months ago, when Mandeep told me that if I wanted to, I could re-engage in that relationship.

M. R.: I remember telling him, 'I am feeling secure now, and if you want to reconnect with this person, I am absolutely fine.' I could sense that there was a feeling of loss on both their ends. I did not want to be in the middle of it.

S. S.: I tried keeping in touch with the other person. However, it was hard for him and hence he was not very responsive during that time. But when I asked him if we could get back together, he just came back to my life in a flip. I am taking it slow this time, so we are not rushing into anything.

ON JEALOUSY AND CO-LOVERS

A. G.: *Sidharth, what was the experience of falling in love with this person?*

S. S.: The experience was very different from how it happened with Mandeep. He is in the fashion and acting space. What attracted me to him is the fact that he cooks, loves to feed people, and is very hospitable. For me, this relationship started off as one very sexual in nature. After a year of knowing him, it shifted. So, love happened with this person after a long time. It's taken its course—not like the earlier times. He was very curious about where I'm from. He's never been to the south of India. So there has been a lot of conversations around food, culture, and language. I am on Grindr. But that's just a place for hook-ups for me and I have clearly stated that in my profile. It is not a place where I'm looking for polyamory. Nor am I actively seeking polyamorous people. If encounters happen naturally and then they turn into something else, I let that happen.

A. G.: *Do you feel jealous, Mandeep?*

M. R.: So, for me, jealousy was, for the longest time, a marker of love. I thought if I felt jealous, it was because I loved the person. Till I began to understand that being jealous in any situation is unhealthy. It happened when I began to resolve my issues with my father that had led me to chase unavailable men and feel jealous. I began to think of jealousy as a symptom of something not being quite right with myself, in myself. Mostly, it has nothing to do with the partner or even the third person that you are jealous of. It has to do with something that you're feeling about yourself. So, I take a pause. Maybe there's a conversation in the relationship that I need to have, or maybe it's an internal conversation. These days it's become rare though. But if it happens, I know it comes at a key moment when maybe something isn't quite right with the way I feel about myself.

S. S.: But, for you, it's a bodily experience, isn't it?

M. R.: Yes, I can feel it, like a surge of jealousy flows through me. A couple of years ago, when I was down with a very bad bout of typhoid and Sidharth was pursuing something with another person, I felt it so strongly. I think it happens when I am physically weak and my immunity is low. I saw Sidharth behave very differently with him. He would smoke because the other guy smoked. He even smelled alien. And he was listening to songs that were their songs. These changes in him were beginning to make me insecure. There was another time I remember, when he had come home from being with someone else and he came to hug me. I just could not do it. My body pushed him away. I felt the other person was still on his skin.

S. S.: My feelings of jealousy come from feeling insecure about myself. And it doesn't occur with all the boys that Mandeep is interested in, but particular ones who I think are threats. They are from the arts world where I find myself an outsider, including those who are doing independent professional work. It is not a threat to the relationship but a threat to me as a person. It's basically me judging myself and battling with my own feelings of inadequacy. But this is something that is changing over time, as

I'm feeling more confident of myself, my interests, my likes, my talent—everything. I'm slowly making peace with it. The constant dialogue with Mandeep helps a lot. However, I must say I don't let myself stay jealous. I get curious when Mandeep mentions someone. I ask a lot of questions and probe, which can make him irritated sometimes. I also stalk them on social media, find out more about them, do my research, and satisfy myself. I don't feel it in a bodily way. My heart does not sink or anything. Once I find out enough about them, I feel better. So, the feeling of jealousy does arise but I work on it and remove the feeling.

A. G.: *Do you see jealousy as something caused by an invasion of what is your possession?*

M. R.: (It's) Not possessiveness as much as not being able to participate in your lover's life when you want to. So, the incident I was talking about earlier, when I had typhoid and Sidharth was interested in someone, comes to mind again. Sidharth was, at that time, sharing his house with the other person. And then Sidharth had to move to Coimbatore. I wanted to be around when he was packing stuff and cleaning out, but I could not because the other person was there. And then on this other person's Instagram, I see some suitcases being packed. It felt really bad, not being able to participate in this important moment.

S. S.: I could have been more sensitive that time, I know. In my head, I was open about everything to Mandeep, so I had sort of absolved (myself of) all responsibility. But I did not realize this was hurting him.

M. R.: I think that was a big moment for our relationship. I remember sitting in a taxi and saying to him, 'Why do you not see my anger, my hurt?' Maybe I was more adamant because I had typhoid and was physically very weak. He had gone on a holiday with this person. And even when I had told him I didn't want to see this person, he had brought him home straight from the airport—right into my living room. All this added up. So, we spent many days talking about how he was not able to see what I was experiencing. His argument was that he was being honest.

But honesty has burdens too, that other people have to bear. It took us a long time to figure this out.

S. S.: That was probably the first time that we had a really difficult strain on our relationship. It was two years ago.

ON STRUGGLES

A. G.: Are there still struggles in your relationship with respect to practising polyamory?

S. S.: For me, sometimes, it is a struggle around communication with the other person. That's because I don't want to hurt anyone. I just like to always be as open as I can be. But sometimes I am careful around communication with the other folks. Also, I have learnt to share as much as Mandeep wants to know and not flood him with information.

M. R.: There are struggles but I feel we convert them into conversations. I guess the initial struggle for me was when I saw Sidharth building alliances that weren't only sexual in nature. We knew that we had to have a conversation if that happened. When the conversation did not happen, I struggled. But I guess the struggle ends because he is always open for a dialogue. He is now seeing another person as we told you, and recently he asked me very sweetly, 'This thing is going on and you don't seem to be saying anything about it—so are you okay with it?' I wasn't thinking about it, but for me, just that check-in helps immensely. To know that he's thinking about how I feel about it.

S. S.: Another aspect of the struggle is that I'm learning to not give my opinion about people to Mandeep at the very start, even if I know them a little. I now wait for him to tell me. We can have a laugh about it later if anything happens. But if I see something that I feel is not going to work out or that could damage something between us, then I will still definitely speak out and protect our relationship.

M. R.: I would also like to say that in this dynamic of polyamorous relationships, we are navigating around other people too.

Sometimes I feel the need to also protect other people from a lack of confidentiality that may happen between us. This is something we have to keep in mind. I will point out that specific information cannot go out. This is about my close sexual encounter with someone and I am sharing it with you because you are my lover but it is with extreme confidentiality. We have to treat it like that.

ON COMING OUT AS POLYAMOROUS

A. G.: From promiscuous to shallow to fickle to frivolous—we have been called many things. How do you feel about being out as polyamorous and how do you negotiate with the world?

M. R.: All my struggles, including about my sexuality, have been with family. The world accepts more readily who I am and gives me love. Right from when I came out as gay to my parents and friends, I decided that I needed to be okay with myself and the world would be okay. And I've seen that happen. People are okay with it. There's enough distance. I am someone else's son. It doesn't matter to them. Within my family, it's been a huge struggle. My father won't even look at Sidharth. While my mother is very friendly with him on her own, if she is with my father, she will not acknowledge him. It's been twenty-three years since I came out to them. And even now we deal with some horrors. I was bringing up my nephew with my parents for eight years. But one day my father forbade him from being around Sidharth for the child's 'safety'. He associated gay people with paedophilia. My struggle really has been with my family and I don't think I will open up to them about being polyamorous any time soon. If they know they know. I have realized that if they have discomfort around any of the choices that I have made, that discomfort is theirs and it has nothing to do with me.

A. G.: Sidharth, what do the world's opinions mean to you?

S. S.: In the beginning, when I was starting to accept that probably I am polyamorous, I spoke about it to people. But there was a lot of judgement. Strangely, cis gay men had more issues with it than straight men and have called me really vile things. These are friends, queer people. There's a lot of bashing that includes, 'Oh, you're so shallow,' or 'You're just a sex maniac,' or 'You have a partner, then why are you looking?' etc. I guess gay people perhaps want to replicate the mono family unit and polyamory disturbs that notion. The heterosexual people, in this case, find my life more amusing, more thrilling, more liberating. A gay person once said that I was just 'trying to be' a hyper-evolved sex-positive person.

A. G.: Do you introduce yourself as a polyamorous person?

S. S.: I don't introduce myself as a polyamorous person immediately. But if someone asks me, I say, 'Yes I am.' It's usually after a sexual experience, or when they probably have an interest in me and they already know I have a partner. I have shared this with my sister too, and while she does not quite understand, she is fine with it. I would say I assess people before I share this information. If I feel there will not be any judgement, then I share.

ON PRIMARY RELATIONSHIPS

A. G.: How did you understand that you were primary for each other?

M. R.: I guess in our case, 'primary' is defined by the fact that we're living together, sharing space.

S. S.: But Mandeep, we've decided to live together. We've taken so many years to get to that, with so much work.

M. R.: But I'm saying that at this given moment, if we wanted to deprioritize this relationship—we wouldn't be able to do that because we're living together. By default, it becomes a primary relationship then.

S. S.: This living together is something I'm still navigating because the first five years of the relationship we had our own spaces.

M. R.: Yes. We have just one room. We have a two-room apartment but I have an Airbnb in one of the rooms, so we only have one room to live in.

S. S.: He has been nice, because early on, I told him that hey, listen, if we fight, you can't ask me to actually leave the house because I don't know where to go. You can go downstairs to your parents. I can't. While we have never had that situation, I do feel sometimes that this is not my home.

M. R.: And since my parents live downstairs, they don't make it easy for him either. To go back to your question, I guess, one way to look at what 'primary' really means is in the language of caregiving. The primary caregiver is the person who's there to catch you when you fall—the immediate person. The one responsible, the one who is going to take you to the hospital, change your diapers.

S. S.: For me, it's not just that. It's also about the social space—whom you appear with in society. In this day and age, it's important.

M. R.: But you can appear in different circuits with different people, I guess. Also, could it be a question of how we define what is 'primary'? Is it emotionally primary or physically primary—could those be different? I guess there is a whole spectrum of what different people understand as 'primary'.

A. G.: *Do you think either of you could have another relationship that could become primary?*

S. S.: I have not been able to reach that level of emotional connection with anyone else. It could be because I have not explored. I guess one would need to live with a person to explore this side. But right now, I can't think of anyone else as the primary person in my life.

M. R.: I'm already thinking about that. I don't think we've spoken about it, but the fact that we were toying with the possibility that we may be living in different cities when you were talking about moving to the south....

S. S.: But it's not happening now.

M. R.: It's not happening now. But I was already, in my head, preparing ground for the fact that equally important relationships could happen and then am I okay with that? In fact, that's when we had the conversation about Sidharth going back to pursuing the relationship that he had paused for me earlier. I felt that if there's a possibility of moving to different cities, then we must make space for such relationships. I think it's quite important for our romantic and sexual health. That's what really opened me up to telling Sidharth to follow his heart with this other person. Let's begin to open up that possibility. It was liberating for me.

S. S.: I think I've not even given a thought to having another primary. Maybe because I am not someone who can foresee these things. I just need to be in the process to figure it out. For now, I can't think beyond Mandeep as a primary partner.

M. R.: Strangely, I can. Even though I haven't yet had a romantic relationship with another person as deep as the one I have had with Sidharth, within polyamory.

5

BOAT OF HOPE II
'MY IDEA OF LOYALTY IS COMMITMENT
TO MAKE IT WORK'

Shankar (name changed) is in his late forties and lives between India and America. He is a researcher and scholar and teaches graduate students. He uses he/him as his pronouns. He has been living as a polyamorous person for a long time. His partners live in different countries, which poses additional challenges for him. We discussed many aspects of living as a polyamorous person and its various high and low points. I have known him for a short while but spent much time discussing various issues in the practice of polyamory. I find Shankar's ways of seeing, experiencing, and participating in the world unique and empathetic. Here are excerpts from our conversation.

A. G.: I want to start with your discovery of polyamory. How did it all begin?

S: I wouldn't say I discovered polyamory; rather that I discovered its language. I was born polyamorous because I never understood being mono. But I didn't have the language to express it then. In school and college, we just said 'open relationship', and it was quite common then. Sometimes, I think we are getting more conservative now. But around 2005, I discovered the language and started to understand the meanings of this practice. Oh, by the way, Happy Metamour Day.

A. G.: Happy Meta Day to you too, Shankar. I did not know it was a thing, and that it was today!

S: Metamour Day falls on 28 February. Valentine's Day is on

14 February. A metamour is twice the love, so 14x2=28 was chosen. Well, to continue—with the language, I also discovered the community. At that time, we would be hiding behind the internet and trying to seek each other out, making virtual communities all over the world. The internet was a real blessing, you know—we could at least find and support each other while living in a world where we were ostracized.

A. G.: Yes, I remember that time and those various communities and chat rooms. So where do you stand today with your polyamorous life?

S: Those days, when we said we were in open relationships, it meant we had one partner, and the others we had relationships with were not 'partners'. However, I soon moved to polyamory, where there were multiple relationships and multiple partners, and my partners too had multiple relationships and multiple partners. Maintaining these various relationships is harder in some ways. But for me, this works much better. I have figured that while I like sharing about my relationships with other partners, there are many who don't like to share that much. Or even hear about other relationships. There is a matter of consent here. So I have learnt to ask if it is alright to share, and if so, how much, and where the limits are. We all have different ways of how we deal with insecurity and jealousy. Just because someone is polyamorous does not mean that they are all sorted and have dealt with their issues. So that's how my journey has been.

A. G.: You live in two continents so far from each other. I know you travel a lot in between. Does the distance bring difficulties?

S: Long-distance relationships are challenging, whether they are mono or poly. Each relationship has its own dynamics—how to keep in touch, how we spend time apart, how we keep the other in our thoughts—it's different in each case. Everybody has their own preferences for communication—frequency, mode, what they like to talk about, what they don't like to talk about. Things change on virtual platforms. Being physically present is different from communicating on text message, phone calls, video calls.

The additional problem is the difference in time zones. The feeling that I can't be there for my partners when I want to and they can't be there for me—it is tough. Some people, over time, figure it out. Some struggle. I am yet to figure it out.

I think, at this point, I identify more as a relationship anarchist than as polyamorous. I believe that relationships with each person should be customized. We shouldn't take the 'one size fits all' that society wishes on us. Children grow up with this mindset; it is indoctrinated in them. They think you have to be on a relationship escalator—like one thing must lead to the next. Dating, falling in love, marriage, babies—that's life. The only life. That's how insidious the social programming is. There is a lot to unpack when one grows up. This conditioning is there in books, movies, all kinds of popular culture that is fed to us. It's just like how American kids rarely learn about the genocide of Native Americans. They are even told that Africans forcibly brought to the Americas were migrant labourers and not slaves! Similarly, one is taught not to question monogamy, marriage, or the idea of having children.

I am also an anti-natalist, i.e., against the human race growing any more. I believe we humans are an overpopulated species using up the world so fast. We're destroying other species; we're destroying the environment. So I believe that humanity should non-violently reduce our population levels. The most non-violent way to do this is to have less or no children. I have nothing against people who have kids. It's just that I don't want to add to it. Wealth from parents, I think, should not be given to children, but to the poorest of society through charity after one's death. That way we can create some form of parity. So anti-natalism is the core tenet of my relationship anarchy. It makes it difficult in partnerships. It is surprising how many people take offence to this philosophy.

In relationship anarchy, one does not need to have one's own children. You can be a co-parent with someone who has had kids with other partners. Like you can be a romantic partner with somebody, and share home with somebody else. And they don't have to all be the same kind of partner. I believe it's important that we get to build multiple close or intimate relationships. Many people do have them without consciously choosing to. My current philosophy incorporates some of this, based on the relationship anarchy 'smorgasbord'. It's a Swedish word meant for a wide variety of food that is put on a table. Googling 'relationship anarchy smorgasbord' shows many different ways in which one can consciously create close and supportive relationships in their life.

A. G.: *What are some of the negotiations, discussions, rules, and boundaries that you think of when you're getting into a relationship? How do you frame these?*

S: For a relationship anarchist, this changes from relationship to relationship. Earlier, I would have one process for all the people I met, and applied it to every relationship; but I realized that it doesn't work. People require different amounts of time to process things, and different levels of consent on what is expected to be shared, so that it doesn't trigger them.

Sometimes you land up doing things you don't want to. Once, a mono partner wanted me to be mono, and I did it for some time. But in my head, I was resentful. I think, at times, I was passive-aggressive. Looking back, I think it was really wrong of me to do that. I have realized now I cannot do mono. There was also once someone who was polyamorous and wanted to have polyamorous relationships, but wanted me to be mono. She had other partners who accepted that. Again, I have nothing against consenting adults making that choice, but I can't do it. So, a whole lot of things do need discussions and figuring out, relationship to relationship.

A. G.: *I think it is very important to have that clarity. And with it, the honesty to accept what we can and cannot do. What do you think is the role of honesty in your relationships?*

S: The concept of honesty was really important to me until somebody pointed out that we actually lie without realizing it. Say, if someone bought something very expensive, wore it, and asked me how they looked in it—and if I thought they did not look nice, I would still hesitate to say that. I would probably find a way to compliment their purchase, just so that they don't feel awful about something they cannot change. Maybe I should be honest and give my real opinion, but I think sometimes, it is more important to be nice rather than right. We make up all these lies without realizing it. I've learned to stop beating myself up over that, you know.

Some things we tell our partners to make them feel good—and I think that's okay. We must remain honest about the big things—the important things. Say about relationship boundaries, or maintaining a partner's trust. These are places where one must be honest. But one has to respect what a partner wants, too. I had a partner who said that she did not want to hear anything about my past relationships. I felt it was a weird request, and I didn't understand it at first. But we kept those boundaries. Then I introduced her to one of my friends, and she got close to that person, who, without realizing it, gave her a whole rundown of my past relationships. That somehow brought out some deep-seated insecurities and complicated things for us.

A. G.: *You mentioned jealousy and insecurities earlier. Do you feel jealous of others? Do your partners feel jealous? How do you manage?*

S: Unfortunately, I tend to be the jealous one. For the longest time, I think I was lying to myself that I didn't feel any jealousy. I had told myself that I've overcome jealousy, I'm not insecure, and all that stuff, which is not true. It's a human thing, we all feel it. But when I do feel insecurity or jealousy, I try not to let it affect my partner. I try to reflect on it and figure out how to manage it.

I like listening to the things that my partners are doing with their other partners, and I too want to do those things that make my partner happy. Jealousy, for me, kicks in when a partner does something with another partner that they don't like doing with me. So, then I ask myself why this is so important to me. For example, if a partner with whom I have communication issues, has excellent communication with somebody else, like they finish each other's sentences—I struggle with that. But the issue is not them—it is with my own shortcoming. That I can't communicate well enough, or I don't understand my partner well enough. Then I feel that I must work on my communication. It is a learning opportunity for me, rather than a reason to be angry at someone else.

A. G.: Now that you have spoken about your co-lovers or metamours, what has been your relationship with the partners of your partners?

S: Often, my partners don't want me to know or hang out with my metas. I don't know why that is. I think we'd get along pretty well; after all, we do love the same person. But if that's a boundary my partners want, then I have to respect it. I have met some of them while dropping a partner off at theirs—but never spent too much time. In a few rare cases that I've got to spend time with them, I have built lifelong friendships with them. Even after I have broken up with our common partner or they have, we have maintained independent friendships. That has been nice. But I don't know the vast majority of my metas. That's unfortunate, and I wish I had closer relationships with them.

A. G.: What have been some of the most difficult things you've had to struggle with in polyamory?

S: Utter disapproval from everyone. You get attacked all the time. You get called all sorts of names. It's been pretty bad. I don't know how to explain it really. Especially mono people just don't get it. I think all poly people have experienced it when they share their beliefs with mono people. Often the first thing mono people think about is sex, and you get labelled as a sexual deviant. It's not just about sex; it's about the relationship. In the polyamorous community, asexual relationships are fairly common.

On the other hand, sexuality is also stigmatized in society today. Surprisingly, a country like the US that is seen as open and progressive, is actually very conservative. Even more than India sometimes. I feel more accepted in India than I am in the US for my polyamorous life and relationship-anarchist views. I feel religious fundamentalism in both countries, and all over the world, has suddenly taken off, and is controlling so much in society. I worry the world is getting more conservative each day. It is to our detriment, because the way they interpret religion leaves no space for polyamorous people. Even though several religions used to be okay with polygamy—if you read the Bible, or several old scriptures of different religions, they say humans were not mono. But then patriarchy kicks in, and only men are allowed to have multiple partners.

A. G.: True. Society's judgement of polyamorous people can be really harsh. But what about the difficulties you have struggled with in your polyamorous relationships?

S: My own jealousy, for sure—(the feeling) that my metamours are better than me. Improving communication or improving understanding of my partner. Also, time is a big difficulty. Especially when I am living across two countries. The other struggle is if I get attracted to a mono person. The thing is, you can't help who you're attracted to. While mostly, I get into relationships with poly folks, sometimes I fall in love with a mono person. That is challenging. Relationships between mono and poly people are very, very difficult. I keep telling all my polyamorous friends—don't do it, just don't do it.

A. G.: What do trust, loyalty, security mean for you as a polyamorous person?

S: I think the big word for me is commitment. In the mono world, commitment means one won't have sex with somebody else. It's easy for an asexual person or somebody who doesn't have a libido. But for an allosexual person—someone who regularly feels sexual attraction—one would ask, why is this your idea of commitment? I found that in the case of most mono people that I have met, if they have sex with someone other than their partner, they end up liking that person better, and they will leave the first partner. I think there is a Johnny Depp quote that if you are in love with two people, then choose the second. I find it very offensive. It assumes that you only fall in love with another person if you have no love left for the first person. Why do you have to choose? If you love two people, accept that you love two people, and continue to love two people.

My concept of commitment is to be with the person for the long haul. I'm committed to making this work. No matter what happens. That's my idea of loyalty too. It doesn't matter who my partner has sex with or has feelings for or loves—I will be there. When they need me, I will make it a point to be there. It's more difficult when you're in two countries, and have other responsibilities. But I try my best. No matter which other people enter their lives, or my life, I will make it a point to make the relationship work.

A. G.: Are there doubts or questions you have about polyamory that you are still working on?

S: There is one. There is a concept of DADT—Don't Ask Don't Tell. In polyamorous communities, there is debate on whether this is ethical. In one such group, someone said that, it's always unethical. Another person in the group argued that saying it is unethical comes from a position of privilege. For example, gender privilege, or economic privilege. Those who don't have it may be forced into not telling for the fear of what would happen to them. Also, if two people decide that's what works for them, then why should anyone decide what is unethical? Would it be my preferred form of relationship? I don't think so. I definitely like to hear about my partner's relationships as well as share my own experiences. But I cannot judge what other consenting adults choose for themselves.

I will give you another example. I know two women who have completely opposing political views. One is a Republican and the other a Democrat. They have agreed to not talk about politics at all. That's the only way they feel the relationship can work. Their friends, from both political camps, attack them constantly. As in, how can they sleep with the enemy?! Questions come up because politics is such a core value for us. But it works for them. It is a difficult area and I don't have clear answers.

A. G.: What values does being polyamorous bring to your life? What have you gained in life being polyamorous?

S: Our mono-normative films and TV sometimes see insecurity, jealousy, and suspicion as virtues—even as indicators of love, rather than challenges to face. Several mono people just unquestioningly live with them and never learn to overcome them. Polyamory has helped me face my own insecurity and jealousy, and dealing with it has helped me become a better person.

Loneliness has become a problem in our society today, with several countries declaring it an epidemic. One of the difficulties is that we've moved away from our traditional communal living into isolated small mono nuclear families. Dana Adam Shapiro, after interviewing married mono couples all over the world, came to the conclusion that only 17 per cent of them are happy. I think I've rarely to never felt lonely, and I'm mostly happy with my life and relationships. I ascribe that to being a polyamorous relationship anarchist.

SAILING WITH MANY LOVES

Somudro toh buro hoyechhen
Pither upore kawto bhari dweep o pahar
Obhijatri, tomar noukay
Khelnar pray
Shonkoch korona tumi, oituku bhaar
Onayashe somudro ke diye deowa jaay

(The ocean has grown old
On its back the weight of so many islands and hills
Traveller, your boat is
But a toy
Do not hesitate, that meagre weight
Can be given quite easily to the ocean)

—Joy Goswami (translation by Arundhati Ghosh)

6

CRAFTING A LIFE OF MANY LOVES: PRACTICE, PRACTICE, PRACTICE

Imagine you are in your living room, where a few friends have come over for an evening of adda. Everyone is speaking at the same time. It's warm, cosy, and lovely. But you, as host, must make sure you listen to all of them. It's hard. No matter how much we talk about multitasking, being able to listen to many voices at the same time is difficult business, even if they are utterly beautiful. So is crafting a life of many loves, even when each one of them brings you considerable joy. But neither is impossible. In my exploration of polyamory over the years, and the many conversations I have had with people from the community, I have understood that one can unlearn the various trappings of a monoamorous world into which we are conditioned. One can participate in rediscovering fresh ways of living that requires effort, rigour, patience, and perseverance. When there are a lot of voices speaking, one learns to listen more keenly. Some friends joke that since I have raised funds for the arts and culture most of my life, these qualities come easy to me. I tell them that fundraising has taught me two other important things—firstly, to continuously keep asking, and secondly, to always receive rejection with grace! But, like any new adventure, making a polyamorous life work in the best way requires—more than anything else—commitment to its practice.

JEALOUSY

Whenever I begin a conversation on how polyamory works, I am asked, 'Are you never jealous?' with a mix of curiosity and scepticism. This is the most important aspect of polyamory that puzzles others—the apparent lack of jealousy. The short answer—of course I am jealous! How can I not be, given my conditioning in a heteronormative one-true-love universe where jealousy is not just evidence but the absolute measure of love! A lover I once had would complain if I wasn't jealous—'You don't love me enough' was his accusation. The K. M. Nanavati v State of Maharashtra case of 1959 comes to mind, where Kawas Manekshaw Nanavati, a naval commander, was tried for the murder of Prem Ahuja, his wife's lover. The incident received unprecedented media coverage, with support for Nanavati, and inspired several books and films where Nanavati's jealousy was justified and his actions celebrated. When I was growing up in the '90s, harassing, bullying and physically assaulting a woman, including throwing acid on her face, had become commonplace if she left a lover and took on another. Even today, there is plentiful news of jealous spouses killing their partners—intimate partner violence is abundant. There is a softer and sympathetic undertone when people talk about jealous lovers being violent towards themselves or their partners. In the world of monoamory, the feeling of jealousy is not just celebrated but considered inevitable. Jealousy is there in polyamory too. But what is also practised is not allowing jealousy to fester into an incurable wound, torment the partner with it, or permit it to be the reason for the end of an otherwise wonderful relationship.

I have had strong experiences of jealousy that were both visceral and deeply physical in nature. It would gnaw at my heart, slowly eating away all the good thoughts in a relationship. Some days it would boil and bubble in my stomach, getting sharper, more caustic. Its bitter-bile taste would rise up and sting my mouth. On other days, it would fill me up quickly with a blind rage and dark grief and leave me in a stormy haze. I would feel like I was drowning—unable to breathe, my chest about to explode. These bouts of jealousy even made me physically ill on some days. I have spent too many nights in pitiful states myself and tortured lovers over them. But as I started digging deeper into these feelings of jealousy, I realized that firstly, it can be identified and tamed, and secondly, it is an utterly futile emotion producing nothing but self-destructive toxins. I also learnt that it is immensely possible to practise accepting it, controlling its damage, and in time, dispensing with it altogether. But first, it is important to understand why we feel jealous.

Jealousy is not a single emotion and the reasons why we feel it when our partners are intimate with others, differ from person to person. Many psychoanalysts have studied it for ages. I, too, have found a few answers in my long and arduous exploration of jealousy. Some people see the partner as a possession. 'You are mine' has made for the lyrics of many popular songs, establishing the idea of 'no trespassing'. Much like the legal rights over private property, 'loyalty' rights prevail over the lover. If one understands this, it is easy to see here why monogamy evolved with the advent of private property as discussed in an earlier chapter. There are others who see the partner fused to themselves—an extension of their own being. 'Ek ho gaye hum aur tum (You and I have become one)' from *Bombay* (1995), and lyrics of that nature, take songs to the hit charts. Here, the intimacy of another person with the partner becomes a nonconsensual intimacy with the self. This creates a sense of violation which is strongly resented.

Some people also fear being displaced. They imagine that the partner might 'replace' them with another. Unable to see space for multiple loves in a person's life, in them, jealousy creates the illusion of the heart as a room with only one chair. This reason for jealousy is often accompanied by feelings of insecurity and inadequacy. Insecurity, because one already starts feeling and performing the sense of being abandoned by the lover; and inadequacy, because one blames the self for not being 'good enough' and that is seen as the reason for the partner being intimate with another person. I have been more jealous of my partner's other partners when I have known that they brought something into their life that I cannot. Whether it is riding a motorcycle and going for adventures, playing a sport they love, developing scholarly arguments together, or even knowing a certain mother tongue—in places where I know I fall short, jealousy grips me tight in its claws. This reason becomes debilitating because the feeling moves quickly from anger against the partner to self-pity and self-loathing.

There is yet another reason why we feel jealous. We are often fuelled by a sense of competition—wanting to always be No. 1, sit at the centre of the universe. Due to unempathetic parenting, we grow up assessing our own worth only through the extent of our achievements and acquisitions. We see our parents smile only when we bring home a prize, so we embed in ourselves the idea that we matter only when we win something. We learn to despise loss. When our partners are intimate with others, we suffer from a sense of having lost them and that makes us angry, taking a toll on our self-worth.

Is jealousy natural or constructed? We are made to understand that it is a natural feeling. But just like heteronormativity or monogamy, I believe it is at least partially constructed. Monoamorous love presented to us in stories, songs, films, books, and in the manner in which people behave, teaches us to be jealous. However, I feel it does not matter whether it is natural or constructed, because when one chooses the polyamorous life, one must learn to manage jealousy and if possible, over time, eliminate it from one's life.

So how do we manage jealousy? In my own life, I have decided that I will not be afraid of this painful emotion. When I feel jealous, I follow a simple routine. I first try and understand the reason for it and accept it without trying to 'conquer' it. I let it flow through me and settle. The heartburn is horrible—a bit like drinking neem juice—but it's okay; it's good for health. I attempt to remember the love I experience with that partner, and recall that I know their heart is large enough to accommodate more than one person. I have found that the best way to cope is to restrain myself from blaming the partner, and instead, telling myself, 'This is how I am feeling and this feeling is my responsibility.' I know that I can also ask for my partner's help. So sometimes, I share my feelings with my partner, if I feel they will listen with patience. One of the worst ways to experience jealousy is to do so without any protection or safety net from the partner. Again, it is important that we share this feeling without accusation, and while they should listen with care, they should do so without feeling guilty. This depth of trust comes with time and communication. Every time I have come out of one of those hellish spiralling jealousies, I have felt liberated and alive.

There are ways to support a partner's jealousy too, especially when they are not good at handling jealousy on their own, or have not had enough practice doing so. Listening to their fears and fumes without judgement is the first and hardest step. They may doubt our love, disregard all the good things in the relationship, blame us for feeling miserable, or burden us with guilt—it is important to listen with kindness and not react to the outpouring of emotions. Reassurances sound very empty at this time. But after the haze of it has passed, I have found partners remembering and acknowledging my support. The worst way to help a lover is to get all rational on them at this point, or justify one's actions, or even recall agreements one has made in the relationship that do not have any space for jealousy. Jealousy is not a rational affair; it is an emotion that needs to play itself out, especially by those who are new in the craft of managing it. Waiting patiently, with a ready and steady shoulder for leaning on, is the best way for a partner to walk through this difficult region.

I continue to feel jealous in some situations, but its impact is much reduced now, as I continue to train myself to respond differently. Polyamorous people don't speak of jealousy enough. They should. It shows our vulnerable side. That way, we won't be seen as freaks but as folks struggling through it all, just like our monoamorous friends.

Being monoamorous, however, does not protect one from jealousy. In the worst-case scenario, people end up having secret affairs that don't stay secret. They burst into the lives of unsuspecting victims with copious amounts of toxin aided by silly mistakes like unmindfully picking up a spouse's phone when a secret lover calls. And jealousy wages a devastating war on the relationship. In the best-case scenario, where partners actually keep to their promise of not being intimate with others, there are still strong jealousies about parents, siblings, friends, or even hobbies that engage the partner. I have seen people being jealous of their partners spending time with a whole range of things and people, including motorcycles, bee hives, work colleagues, and even their own children! Intimacy, like love, can have different meanings for different people. The ruins of these various jealousies are all quite overwhelming. The only way to live with jealousy is to practise all the different ways in which polyamorous people negotiate their relationship with it.

Is it possible to have 'clean love'—devoid of jealousy or expectations, like Buddhism preaches? I am sure it is possible for some people if they practise hard enough. But for me, the struggle is a reality. I cope on some days and I don't on others. But each day I accept working with jealousy a part of my practice.

COMPERSION AND CO-LOVERS

One of the wonders, and also demands of resisting conventional ways of living is that you must explore new ways of articulating where there is no language known to you. In my search for the opposite of jealousy, I stumbled upon the word 'compersion'. It is understood as the joy someone feels when their partner receives love and pleasure from another partner. The partner of a partner is known as a 'metamour' in polyamorous parlance, but I like the word 'co-lover' better; so that's what I use. Compersion is the Holy Grail that is pursued eagerly by many of us in polyamory. But between jealousy on one end of the spectrum and compersion on the other, most of us find ourselves somewhere in the middle, hopefully working our way towards compersion. But even the work in progress is hard. 'I am happy for my lover who is enjoying a holiday with another lover' is not a thought that's easy to internalize, accept, or exercise. However, rationally, if one contemplates on what love, even in its most conservative sense, is professed to be, it is being 'happy for the one you love'. The idea of compersion only stretches this to include the 'co-lovers' in the mix. But emotionally, it takes a lot of work.

In my case, I have noticed that it works differently for different co-lovers. In places where my own insecurities are higher, or for some reason, I don't like the co-lover much, it is harder for me to move towards compersion. But where I feel comfortable because my relationship with the co-lover is that of trust and mutual friendship, or my lover enables a process of reassurance that I can depend on, I can move towards compersion with more ease. So, it all depends on the person's own mental state and feelings about the self, relationship with the lover, and understanding with the co-lover. Maintaining relationships is so much like baking—the right ingredients, temperature, and time are delicately balanced to create wonders. But any one thing amiss can be disastrous. One needs to listen patiently and hold hearts with gentleness.

Co-lovers face two main problems. For women, there is precedence for this in history, in the co-wives in a polygynous structure of marriage with a polygamous man. While there was some sisterhood and camaraderie in the women's quarters, often, the access to and frequency of presence of the husband in the bedroom did become contentious. Tools of patriarchy were used by both men and women to create competition among the co-wives. In polyamory too, one can slip into that zone easily if one is not careful. Patriarchal values run deep in all of us. For men as co-lovers, the journey is a longer one, since cultures of polyandry are neither spoken about nor represented in our popular culture. I have not heard in the languages that I know—Bangla, English and Hindi—the male version of what in Hindi or Bangla we call a 'sautan' or 'shoteen', meaning the co-wife. As far as the subject of a woman having many husbands is concerned, we only go as far as Draupadi's five husbands, and there too, we ignore the co-lover relationships of the five brothers, completely placing all our attention on the invincibility of their fraternal bonds. So, men have to begin from scratch in terms of living with co-lovers in contemporary polyamorous situations.

However, I have learnt that over time, it is possible to love a person like one loves the inflection in a poem, or edge of the ocean, without having to own that poem or ocean. One can also rejoice when others enjoy them. This sharing of joy is compersion. In some ways, the practice of co-loving in polyamory is also a process of learning to accept, embrace, and celebrate the conventional 'other'—the co-lover.

PRINCIPLES AND COMMUNICATION

Every relationship has some mutually agreed upon terms of engagement. Whether it is spelt out directly or understood quietly, there is always a set of established desires and expectations, ways of behaviour, customs, and reciprocation. It's no different for polyamory. But since these are relationships that have a range of definitions for the different people practising it, the agreements between them can also be quite varied. Polyamory being practised this way is still comparatively new. What is fair to seek, what is beyond its scope, what makes it hard for people to comply with, or what can create ruptures, are still being tested. Thus, often, in polyamory, it is important to expressly articulate the context and frames of reference of the relationship with its specific set of mutually agreed upon ways of interaction. This develops over the period of the relationship. However, most such agreements are created on the foundation of some basic principles which are considered fundamental to the practice of polyamory.

Honesty is the first key principle in polyamorous relationships. There is no place for deception. It starts at the very beginning when we make sure the other person knows that we are polyamorous. From there, depending on the mutually agreed upon rules in that relationship, honest sharing takes place. In most relationships, there is a mutually agreed upon limit on sharing too, where partners decide on how much detail they want to know about the other relationships. This is where the second principle of consent comes in. Since polyamory is a relationship where many people are interconnected through their partners, the consent on sharing must always be vetted by all involved. I cannot share something about one partner with another unless both of them give me consent for it. While many people may think this is a complicated arrangement, I feel that at a time when there is an energized conversation about consent across social circles, polyamory is a great place for the mindful practice of it. It does require work but that work is fuelled by the desire to be just and respectful towards everyone involved.

The reason this consent for receiving information about other relationships is important is also because each one of us is at a different place in our unlearning of jealousies and insecurities. There are anxieties we carry from the conditioning of monoamory, which affect our abilities to cope with details of other relationships. Partners must be considerate. Often, unsolicited or unconsented outpourings of honesty can come out of a need to assuage some hidden guilt. This kind of guilt, too, is a conditioning of monoamory, and it erodes the soul. But this kind of honesty is a heavy load to carry for the partner. A friend once told me that he remains sensitive and alert to the reaction of his partner when he shares information, including praising other partners. Often, sharing memories of an earlier experience of a place or situation that is now again being lived with another partner can trigger unintended comparisons that can be hurtful. I too notice the changing moods of a partner carefully when I share and sometimes restrain myself. If anyone feels that this makes my polyamorous life more arduous than a monoamorous one, I would remind them that I am only as careful sharing details of my present relationships with partners as they are about sharing details of their past ones. The challenges of loving can often bring us to the same difficult crossroads even when we take diverse routes.

Setting of boundaries and giving permission are two other related principles of polyamory. In every such relationship, one must know the definite limits one must not cross and those which are negotiable. These could be a list of people that one does not want the partner to engage with romantically or sexually, which includes close friends or family; activities or areas that are out of bounds; aspects of relationships that must remain private and cannot be shared; and sometimes—especially when there is a primary partner—the extent of intimacies that can be engaged in, with other partners. Boundaries are also created in order to maintain the dignity of each relationship and protect it from inadvertent interferences from others. The negotiable boundaries, however, can change, depending on the journey of the existing relationships and emergence of new ones.

Communication is another very important element in polyamory. With multiple moving parts in the interconnected relationships, it is absolutely crucial to maintain above-board and clear communication between partners. Some relationships are live-in, some are in the same city, but some are also long-distance. We have to manage time with multiple partners. We can't set up dates in a jiffy, or spend a weekend watching sunsets without a plan. A partner could have commitments with other partners. So, we need to be mindful of the openness, limitation, and availability of each partner. Clear communication ensures less scope of misunderstanding and hurt. However, it is sometimes a tall task to always be 'clear'. Especially when it is about the affairs of the heart, and emotions are involved. That's alright. We are human and accept our frailties. As long as there are intentions and efforts to maintain healthy and clear communication, it generally works.

EXPANSIVE SPACE OF REDEFINITIONS

A beautiful aspect of polyamory is that it allows for interrogation and redefinition of many aspects of relationships. For example, we understand loyalty, security, and commitment in very different ways from monoamorous people. I have often seen that in monoamory, the meanings of these words are lodged more in what you will not do with other people outside of the partnership. So, loyalty means you will not be intimate with another person; security means you will not give priority to another person; and commitment means you will not promise anything to another person that you have promised to your partner. The meanings of these words finally rest on references outside of the relationship because monoamory is founded on exclusivity, which demands a strict policy of prohibition. However, in polyamory, we stay within the agreement with our partners; loyalty, security, and commitments are defined within the relationship—loving our partners, caring for them, and being there for them when they need us.

There is also a redefinition of what appreciating a partner means. This is a wonderful though exhausting aspect of polyamory, where one remembers, connects with, celebrates, and communicates the various things that are important to their partners. It would include causes they care about, their politics, festivals they celebrate, languages they speak, interests they are passionate about, and often, people they love and admire. Polyamory thus never allows for narrowing of our ambits of presence or influence. One learns to embrace things that seem alien in the beginning—engage with them, spend time studying them, and understand why they are significant to people who are important to one. Over time, some of these things may become our own passions too. These multiple calls from the world energize me and make my life with more than one person rewarding.

An enriching aspect of polyamory is that its processes enable an ever-expansive space for the definition of love—diverse kinds of love, its meanings and manifestations. So, when something in a relationship of love changes, one does not rush to ask immediately, 'Have I fallen out of love?' but instead wonders, 'Perhaps this too could be love—another kind of love?' There is the realization that one does not 'win' people from others or 'lose' people to them. Each relationship is responsible for itself. It has its own space where nurturing, growing, and transforming each other is continuously active. It's hard to accept this responsibility as we are not taught how to. But it can be learnt and practised.

Sometimes, the same trait in us that is deeply adored by one partner could be the cause of utmost irritability in another. This makes the practice of polyamory a great leveller, refusing to glorify or vilify any one kind of being in love, or any particular way of responding to desires. In love, nothing is good or bad on its own, but fills up with meaning only in relation to the other.

THE SEARCH FOR LOVERS

A friend once jokingly asked me that, in a world where she couldn't find one person good enough to love, how I was finding so many! My response in reciprocated playfulness was that if we stopped looking for 'the one', we would find 'the many'. This is not a trick answer. The list of parameters that we take along with us to find 'the one' is exhausting. It contains not just our needs and desires, but also insurances against all our fears, guarantees against all our insecurities, and ruins of all the dreams others have piled upon us. The list is too long, too heavy, and unbearable in its absurdity. When we do not find anyone matching this list, we turn our hard and critical gaze on ourselves and severely chastise our inadequacy. A similar list is used by others to cast the same sharp judgement on us. This process makes us unkind to ourselves and others, and cynical about love itself. My journey in polyamory has taught me generosity. With that experience, and gratitude for my immense fortune in finding lovable partners, I ask, instead of looking for that elusive 'the one', could one not search for little sparks of hope in people they meet, who could ignite different ways of being together? And could we not keep our hearts open for such encounters to recur? It could make our lives slightly more joyous and a tad less lonely.

7

POLY AT HEART, SOLO IN SPIRIT: THE SINGLE POLYAMOROUS PERSON

A 'solo' polyamorous person chooses to lead a single life, on their own, away from their various partners. This is what I personally identify with the most. Except for the brief period when I was married to a monoamorous person and practised monoamory myself in that relationship, I have never lived in a long-term domestic partnership with anyone. I mention 'long-term' specifically because even short live-in situations—for days or weeks—are forms of sharing the domestic life which comes with its own share of harsh and sweet realities. While I really enjoy having people home—and thus the short stays are frequent between all kinds of partners and friends—the longer, more permanent domestic partnership has not happened for me. Not even with primary partners. I used to think this was accidental. Most of my partners lived settled lives in other cities, and my own frequent and long travel itineraries both for work and pleasure kept me mostly away from home. I must also confess that I have a particularly eccentric living pattern with very odd hours, for which, leave alone others agreeing to cohabit with me, on some days I find living with myself quite unbearable. What I learnt only much later was that the strong desire to be on my own had quietly asserted its will on most of my decisions, including my relationships of love. While, on and off, an intense relationship would have me desire a shared domestic life a little bit, I would soon fold back into my solo existence with great delight and, if I may add, relief.

In more recent years, I have tried to understand what makes me such a joyous solo person who is also deeply polyamorous in my relationships, loving and caring passionately. I spoke with some other people like me to explore this further and I discovered some fascinating details about our lives and why we are this way.

Most of the solo polyamorous people I spoke to absolutely enjoy sharing their time and home with their partners when they visit, and love the comfortable togetherness that comes with growing familiarity over the years. The first few years of the relationships, these days, weeks, or months of spending time together are more of an exciting holiday—experiencing doing things together, like cooking, watching movies, spending hours talking about the subjects that matter, creating sexual intimacies that explore their varied desires, and meeting friends from each other's lives. As years go by, there is more time spent doing the quotidian—work and other chores in the warm presence of each other. And all of them, without exception, shared that after a while, they start missing their solo space. The period of happy coexistence is different for different people, but the craving for having the home to just the self is felt both strongly and recurrently. For me, I have noticed, it is always after a month or so of spending time with partners in my home or theirs that I start missing my solo space. Thankfully, for me, there has been no conflict over this with my partners as they understand it too, and some even feel the same way.

Some solo poly friends of mine stay single because they believe in relationship anarchy. Neither do they prioritize any one partner over the others nor have primary partners. They feel that sharing a domestic space with one of their partners would make them more important in all practical terms, and this would create a hierarchy among their other loves. But the few friends who do have primary partners and yet love their solo lives, find it hard to explain the reasons to others. Even among polyamorous people, we often connect primary partnerships with sharing domesticity. Any deviation from this brings up doubts and misgivings about the depth of love and commitment. But solo poly folks shared how remaining single in their domestic space helps them build a relationship with their own selves and understand who they are without necessarily being influenced by or impacting their relationship with others. A large part of their lives consists of making meanings out of things on their own, conversing with the self, and reflecting and expressing them in some form. A friend blurted out, 'Sometimes, an experience is so personal, so private that anyone being there takes away from its essence.' Do you not want to share it with your partner, I asked. 'I do,' they replied, 'but not just then.'

Some spoke about the 'relationship escalator'—the feeling that once they start living with someone, the anxiety of 'what next, what next?' might immediately take over their lives. Many polyamorous people feel that the moment a domestic partnership is established, the relationship starts to fall into a pattern of pressure much like monoamory, which they have rejected. The comfortable plateau of camaraderie in a relationship that some polyamorous people like me seek—where there aren't destinations or life goals to be achieved together—is most appropriately lived through solo polyamory.

For me, the sense of independence that I manifest in my life is the most important reason for remaining solo. This includes the style and pace of my domestic life, the way my home looks, the various decisions I make on a daily basis, and being able to have relationships as and when I want to. It is hard to make space for 'others' in the home that primary partners share. They often feel stressed or frustrated because they either decide on terms of engagement where they do not bring another person home, or entertain another partner only when their domestic partner is not around.

In polyamory, we choose whether we want to keep our partners separate from each other or introduce them and let things take their own course. These are choices made with mutual agreements. For people living solo in polyamory, this decision is easier in practical terms. One can separate or engage partners at will. But for those who live together, it becomes difficult to keep their domestic partners separate from other partners and maintain distinct relationships.

There is another important reason for me to live solo that some of the people I spoke to agree with. The mind-space one shares with a partner increases with sharing domestic space with them.

'If one person is always there sharing your space; if their life is inscribed within your domestic everyday—then it becomes harder to keep more mind-space free for others,' said a friend who has moved a few times between living with someone and staying on her own while being polyamorous. I agree with that. It has the tendency to look and feel more and more like a monoamorous experience.

Few people talk openly about the financial aspect of living solo as a polyamorous person—as people generally don't like talking about money. Anyone living in this country as a single person will tell you that it is harder financially. Not that family lives are better in this economy of high inflation, but double incomes help in sharing the burden. From rent and utility bills, to buying groceries and eating out—this country is not geared towards letting people be single. The discounts are always on bulk and economies of scale do not favour single lives. For women, the single life often costs more because one pays a premium for staying in 'safe' neighbourhoods and 'safe' housing facilities. Having said that, one of the reasons I chose to live alone is because I believe every person has a certain financial temperament and it is very important for that to match if one is to have a conflict-free domestic arrangement. Financial temperament includes not just spending habits and priorities, but also aspects like risk-taking on investments, attitude towards charity, and overall relationship with money. I have seen many people in domestic partnerships, both in monoamory and polyamory, fight over these financial issues. My need to make decisions about, control, and disburse my finances as I want to without any influence or pressure from a domestic partner is an important reason for my being solo.

A reason that came up almost at the end of a conversation I was having with another solo polyamorous person, struck me as the most beautiful one, full of old-world charm and romance. He said he wanted to live away from his primary partner because he wanted to keep the mystery and attraction alive. He then went on to speak about how much he treasured the longing he felt when he was away from his partner: the skip of the heart when they met after an interval, the flutter in his stomach at the sight of this lover. I was reminded of love poems of Amir Khusrau and Ghalib as I heard him speak. Later, I realized that I felt this way too. The staying away created a sense of 'biraha'—a longing—that kept my relationships more alive and desire more intense. This deprivation of the object of affection creates a deep thirst in me that is hard to explain. In that state of longing, the different methods of communication that connect my partners to me—emails, texts, phone calls, and video chats—add various new dimensions to the discoveries I make of myself and my partners.

Many of these reasons are similar to what monoamorous people experience if they choose to live solo, away from their lover. But the decision to remain solo in polyamory affects more than two lives and must happen with mutual understanding. A question we often have to contend with even if asked in jest is, 'You have more than one lover, and still can't find anyone to live with?'

I tried to connect this with my passion for travelling solo. I am quite an adventurer and love visiting new places, exploring cultures, food, and people. While I like travelling with friends and partners, I absolutely delight in travelling alone. In fact, even when I am travelling with others, I need timeout to go off on my own for a while. This has to do with the deep connection I feel with this world that is immensely personal. I need to be alone with her—in her valleys and waters, as much as her cities and villages. It's an ancient feeling—some may even call it spiritual. Face to face with the all-pervasive life force of the world, each one of us is as truly alone as we are together. Some part of me thus remains solo and some, a piece of the larger collective. I acknowledge and accept both. This liminal space is for me, the authentic self that I celebrate. The moment closest to this feeling is when I return home sad after dropping off a partner to the train station at the end of a wonderful week of live-in together; and the open balcony of my flat, the plants, and warm fairy lights embrace me in gay abandon. I sit. I smile. I am where I belong.

8

NOT FOR THE FAINT-HEARTED: THE CHALLENGES OF POLYAMORY

Sometimes, Ma's response to my practice of polyamory is a Bangla proverb, 'Bhager ma Ganga paina,' which means that after a mother is cremated, her ashes never have the good fortune to be immersed in the holy Ganga (a Hindu ritual that supposedly ensures her safe passage into the nether world) if the responsibility is divided among her many children. The implication is that each one of her children thinks that the other one will do the needful, and ultimately, no one actually does. Ma can be rather cruel when she wants to be. On the other hand, my friends struggling with the demands of monoamory think polyamory is easier. In their imagination, if I have trouble with one partner, I can always seek comfort with another. In a relationship with only one partner, they cannot avail of that option. What they do not understand is that when you have one home on fire, you can't just move residence to another just because there are other homes available to you. You stand there and figure out ways to douse that fire first. From my experience of living both monoamorous and polyamorous lives, each comes with its own fire hazards. We all live with the struggle of love's fragility, its precariousness. But, while all love is hard, polyamory is not a journey for the faint-hearted. What poet Jigar Muradabadi said about love so eloquently, fits perfectly:

Yeh ishq nahi asaan, itna hi samajh leeje
Ek aag ka dariya hai, aur doob ke jana hai

(This love is not easy, understand this much
This is a river of fire, and the way is to dive in)

It is true that some of these difficulties may also be experienced in monoamorous loves, but they get more complex in polyamorous relationships when the number of people and their respective interests in the equations increases.

SHARING TIME AND SPACE

Since, in today's busy lives, it is challenging for even monoamorous folks to spend quality time with their partners and families unless they work hard at it, I have often been asked how I make time for my multiple partners. I have also been asked about the complication of prioritizing among them. But these are not common questions for, say, a mother of three. In that scenario, the proverbial endless love that flows from a woman's heart when she becomes a mother needs no enquiry. But it seems not to apply for people with multiple partners. So, on some days, when I am feeling wicked, I am tempted to say that when a person enters a polyamorous life, they immediately receive an infinite tank of endless love that comes with a lifetime warranty from the Poly-love Goddess. But I don't say that because that would be churlish. Moreover, it is true that in polyamorous relationships, it does get difficult to make time and ensure that one is engaged meaningfully with the various partners. This requires patience and open conversations to arrive at what is feasible and acceptable to each partner. There is scheduling involved and use of calendar, but relationships can hardly be regimented; so, there is a need to check intermittently if everyone is comfortable with the arrangements. These are complicated multi-nodal relationships where the decisions about one affect others. Also, unlike popular assumptions, commitments are real and because they are with different people, one has to be conscious that they are not in conflict. There is a great business opportunity for a good scheduler app that caters to the specific needs of polyamorous people!

A difficult part of polyamory is to understand what kind of time you will *not* be spending with some partners even when you want to. That understanding is very different from the one in monoamorous lives. In monoamory, it is expected and taken for granted that a couple will spend most of their special days together. Whether they are birthdays or anniversaries or important festivals of their communities, couples are likely to spend them with each other and sometimes, their families. However, in polyamory, nothing can be taken for granted. In most cases, important personal and cultural days cannot be spent with all partners, and one has to choose one person for it. It may not be the same partner every time, but when any one partner is chosen, others may sometimes feel a bit unloved unless they cope and process this well. Sometimes, the partner you choose may not consent to spending that time with you for various other reasons, including their commitments to their other partners. Again, since these relationships are not immaculately reciprocal, sometimes my wanting to spend my birthday with a partner and them agreeing may not automatically mean that they also want to spend their birthday with me! In the case of people who have primary partners, it may somewhat hold true, but among others, it does not. This requires adjustment of expectations. This also holds true for taking holidays together and adjusting to schedules that go beyond the partner and involve others in the networks of polyamorous love. Loving is not about measured and equal exchanges, but a way of weathering the liminal spaces between expectations and gratification. Nothing explains as clearly as polyamory that calculations are futile in love.

Sharing space too can be complicated, especially, those who live with nesting partners sharing domesticities. They have to go through a series of difficult conversations with their domestic partner about the boundaries of the use of the home. Many couples only invite other partners when their nesting partner is travelling, or follow a 'don't bring home' policy which requires less adjustments. Among polyamorous folks who do not live with any partner, sharing of their home temporarily, too, can be knotty. The embedded conditioning of monoamory leaves almost invisible traces in all of us and can cause distress due to the visual markers of other relationships present in homes. So, even when I have worked on not being possessive about my partner, I can hold on to being possessive about 'our bed', or feel upset when another partner leaves their toothbrush in 'our bathroom'. These are feelings that need to be engaged with, with kindness and patience, and over time, settled if not overcome.

COPING WITH LONELINESS

Contrary to what people imagine about us with our many partners, in polyamory, one might land up doing many things on one's own. Like I said before, in monoamory, the couple is expected to do things together—often out of choice, and sometimes for optics. In polyamory, our partners may not be there for us when we want to do things together, making us feel lonely sometimes.

Now I have uttered the unmentionable—loneliness. Here is a bogey that we are all desperately running from, a spectre that makes us remain in abusive relationships and hold on to dead marriages, the fear that pushes us to compromise our basic values and ambitions. Loneliness is seen as an affliction for which love is supposed to be the only cure. And finding the one true love is meant to be the enduring talisman against it! I bring up loneliness here because that is the question I have been asked a lot when I discuss polyamory in public. Do I feel lonely because I don't have one exclusive partner all to myself? The truth is I do sometimes, when none of my partners are there to share grief or joy instantly. A friend mentions that even when she has a primary partner, the person may be unavailable, since the nature of commitments here are often different from the habitual togetherness of monoamorous couples. So, what do we do about this loneliness?

Earlier, I used to wonder whether monoamory was a better answer for loneliness. But even monoamory has not found the antidote to loneliness; otherwise, so many people would not feel so lonely in monogamous marriages and have relationships outside, seeking solace. A dear friend who is monogamous told me once that one of the most desolate places in the world is to sleep lonely on one side of the bed shared every night with the same person for years.

The answer to loneliness, for me, lies elsewhere. Loneliness has little to do with how exclusive the partner is or how much time we spend with them. Its core lies in our own sense of inadequacy, and our inability to cope with the failure to be needed, desired, or loved. It comes from a feeling of incompleteness in the self when one does not belong to something beyond the self, something 'more'. We restrict the definition of 'more' to mean another person—almost always, a partner. Without that we feel arid, half-alive. But, in reality, there are many ways to redefine this 'more'—we could belong in the lives of our friends, families, and communities; the neighbourhoods we inhabit; the activities we take pleasure in; and causes we feel passionate about. Apart from this, there is also a need to develop our own sense of esteem and self-worth outside of how much we may be needed by another—something that is intrinsically ours and unaffected by praise or blame for our role in another's life.

And finally, most crucially, one must understand loneliness for what it really is—not a disease to be rid of, or an aberration to be feared—but a human condition, an experience of life just like any other. In fact, feeling a sense of loneliness is a signal to recognize our place in the world, which is both singular and collective.

ADAPTING TO CHANGING DYNAMICS OF RELATIONSHIPS

Since there are multiple people involved in polyamorous relationships, there are many moving parts that keep changing. This makes relationships dynamic. One has to be comfortable to adapt to the shifts that may happen in a relationship. These adaptations may include adjustments one makes to calendars, or to terms of engagement on how much time one spends with each other or whether one travels together or not. But there are also more serious shifts to consider. For example, if one of my lovers has a new lover and naturally wants to spend more time with his new partner to get to know them better, I have to make peace with us spending less time than usual. I also cannot demand that the new lover should automatically like me or fit into our friend circles. On the other hand, my partner needs to be alert to my feelings about this new arrangement and ensure that I don't feel unheard. There are also times when age, illness, financial situation, or mental health issues may require someone to give more time and space to one partner, thus changing the other equations. There may be changes in physical intimacies and sexual relationships. Partners may redefine what their particular relationship will entail and whether sex will be a part of it or not. When these changes are mutually accepted, there may be readjustment issues but no major problem. However, if these are changes that only one of the partners wants and the other feels that they have not been heard, or that they have been coerced—that does not end well. When this seems unfair to one party, there is need for open and honest conversations about the changes.

One of the toughest times in polyamory, for me, has been when, a few years ago, a partner fell in love with someone and decided to become monoamorous. It was tougher because it was not just a question of me grieving the loss and adapting to the new contours of the relationship. He decided to sever all connections with me. The hardest part was that he also left with a value judgement about polyamory as a practice, abandoning a promise made together to create an alternative way of living. But I try not to discuss my heartbreaks caused by one partner, with another. Sometimes, doing so can give an unfair advantage to the one listening. Only after years of being in a relationship have I found the confidence to share the unpleasantness of one relationship with another partner—that too with consent of both partners.

While some of these modifications in relationships may be hurtful, it is important in polyamory to relook at the foundations of relationships from time to time. This helps to understand and separate the feelings of hurt from the actual changes taking place. One can then make space for developments and recalibrate the relationship. I like to draw up broad maps of needs, expectations, and offerings from time to time and share them with my partners, figuring out what works best for us. They don't have to be equal commitments, as long as they are consensual ones. If and when they change, we readjust. But I confess that practising this patiently can be exhausting.

MONO–POLY RELATIONSHIPS

A very difficult situation in polyamory is a relationship between a monoamorous and a polyamorous person. In my opinion, while it may go well initially, soon it turns out to be unfair for both, making it hard for a long-term and joyful relationship to develop between them. But we invariably fall in love with monoamorous people and they, in turn, fall in love with us. Consider Anand Bakshi's famous couplet in *Jab Jab Phoool Khile* (1965): 'Na na karte pyar tumhi se kar baithe; karna tha inkaar magar iqraar tumhi se kar baithe (I fell in love with you while saying no; I should have refused, yet I agreed to be in love with you)'. This seems to be the bane of our lives!

The challenges are manifold in a relationship like that. Firstly, the needs of the two kinds of people are different—where one seeks the security of an ultimate destination in the chosen partner, but for the other this is part of a long and complex journey that will include many people simultaneously. Secondly, what one offers in the relationship is also different. The monoamorous person's fidelity is strictly restricted to this one partner, whereas the polyamorous person remains true to their sense of commitment to their multiple partners. Thirdly, the expectations of shared time and space are different and often conflicting for the two.

A polyamorous person has had to constantly break rules set by society and make space for themselves by redefining not just those rules but also concepts of love and intimacy. A monoamorous person often finds it hard to accept these new definitions emotionally, even if they may understand them rationally and intellectually. The polyamorous person can sometimes come across as too oppositional, too adamant, or too confrontational for the monoamorous person. This excess comes from years of fighting the system, negotiating shame, and unlearning conditioning. This can be overwhelming for the monoamorous person. What often happens in these relationships is that the monoamorous person ends up waiting; brooding; feeling lonely, jealous, and abandoned; and second-guessing the partner—even though they have consented to being in a relationship with a polyamorous person.

This creates resentment and a heaviness of the heart that is difficult to bear. The outpourings, when they come, create tremendous toxicity in the relationship. It becomes unjust for the polyamorous person too. It is wrong to expect a polyamorous person to always be at the receiving end of accusations just because they have chosen to not conform to norms. We tend to be emotionally bullied because we ourselves are on the backfoot with our choices and believe they're our curses to bear. Responsibility of a relationship has to lie with both people. In a mixed relationship like this, if it is important for the polyamorous person to understand the difficulties of the monoamorous person, it is also an imperative for the monoamorous person to learn how to cope with jealousy and other hard feelings.

SLIPPING BACK INTO CONDITIONING

A life that is lived with redefinitions needs to protect itself from going back to old, tried and tested habits. There are so many of these old ways of being that monoamory embeds in us. Jealousy, possessiveness, and fear of abandonment reside side by side with denial, guilt, and shame. When it gets difficult to cope, I have seen people wonder if the mono life is better. Though there is no evidence of any cure for any of these disturbing feelings within monoamory, there is a sense that the jackpot of the perfect partner will make all of our worries vanish. This makes many people give up and move back into monoamorous lives. As long as this happens out of their desire for what they see as a better option for themselves and they are able to abide by the rules of monoamory, there is no problem. But sometimes, wanting the best of both worlds, if they start to sneak out on their partners, then it amounts to cheating.

When polyamorous people slip back into the old patterns of monoamory, especially among primary partners, their demands and expectations start mimicking monoamorous lives. Their polyamorous partners are unable to respond or negotiate, and these relationships become untenable. I have seen how this can become a downward-spiralling tornado.

As a practitioner of many desires, I have fallen, been broken, and failed more than I have rejoiced. I have run towards the safety of the known, the conventional, the doable. Wanting to slip back into monoamory, I have temporarily thought that it was the best solution to stop hurting. However, these feelings have been transient. The recognition that feeling hurt—even excruciating pain—is part of the process of loving someone, is not an easy pill to swallow. And it takes time. What continues to keep me polyamorous is the sheer passion of wanting a world where love is explorative in the many journeys it enables.

BREAK-UPS

Ending any relationship is hard. In polyamory, break-ups between two or more people can happen for various reasons that include physical or emotional abuse, acting without consent, violating the terms of the agreement, and endangering privacy, to name a few. It can also happen due to two people losing compatibility because they have grown apart and differently, or because external situations around them have changed due to job opportunities or new responsibilities. These reasons are not very different from those in monoamory. The difference is that break-ups in polyamory are hardly ever about the open nature of the relationship.

Since, in polyamory, a break-up affects the entire connected chosen family and networks, it poses severe difficulties. In monoamory, too, when a break-up happens there is pressure on friends, family, and close networks to choose a side. Loyalties are questioned and divided, and many more relationships of care and affection in the connected circles are in peril. In polyamory, the circle of the chosen family which is built, in part, due to the discrimination one faces in natal families, becomes very strong and the only place of emotional shelter. Therefore, the question of loyalty can also become quite severe and uncompromising at times.

It is therefore important to remember three things. The first is the responsibility the two or more people breaking up have towards each other; second, the responsibility they individually and jointly share towards their connected circle; and third, the accountability the circle has towards them. Therefore, at the very start, once the decision to part is fixed, the people breaking up must clarify to themselves what this break-up would entail. This is very hard to do when one is feeling all sorts of difficult emotions like hurt, grief, and anger, but unless this is sorted at the beginning, the next steps don't quite work out. This would include figuring out, at least for the time being, whether they would be comfortable sharing space at parties or other common gatherings or whether they would mind the mention of their ex-partners from people in the circle. Since many polyamorous people also open up their boundaries of intimacy, blur the lines, and initiate different definitions for their relationships, it is important to understand what will change and what won't after the break-up. For example, will people still remain friends? Will they continue to have sex? Will they completely cut each other off? Hurt and anger change texture with time and healing, and it is important to review some of these decisions later.

But the most challenging issue is that of common partners. Here I have seen some of my most admired polyamorous people fail to come to a mutually sustainable arrangement. It is one thing to ask a friend or family member to distance themselves from an ex, but to expect a partner to distance themselves from their other partner, with whom you are breaking up, is quite another matter. It becomes too much for most people to be fine with their partners continuing to be a partner of their ex. In the rare case where I have witnessed this work, it has been due to deep trust, resilience, and self-discipline among partners.

It is also important for the circle to remain as non-judgemental as possible and listen to all the many sides in a break-up. It is inevitable that the narratives will not match. It is easy to get into the mode of an arbitrator trying to figure out where the blame lies. But, in my experience, this is best done either by the people who are breaking up themselves or with the help of a professional who is skilled at such analysis. The responsibility of the circle, here, is to be there, hold space, and allow a refuge to the affected people.

In many cases, such break-ups resolve themselves over time. I have seen that people have found ways to change and build different kinds of relationships with ex partners. After all, if they are basically good people who are in love and the reason for the break-up was not abuse of power, then ex-partners can also become important allies as they have known us at some of our worst times.

COMING OUT

It is difficult to establish our identity openly and freely in the face of discrimination. This requires a certain kind of 'coming out'. Like in the queer world, in polyamory, coming out is different for different people, requires various timespans, and has several stages. Since polyamory is still one of the worst taboos, even in otherwise progressive worlds like those of queer people, acceptance is not guaranteed.

We begin with being in denial. I, too, started there. One spends years feeling guilty for what one sees as instability, fickleness, need for attention, or worst of all, inability to form long-term nurturing relationships. Often one does not know that there are other ways of being, so one is very harsh on oneself. But even when one is exposed to polyamory, the ideas embedded in our heads about the splendour of monoamory make us stick to the latter. I know someone who finds it hard to cope with the many loves he has in his life and has labelled some of them 'friends' and said, 'Let us not define too much,' lest these relationships make his current partner uncomfortable. The worry is that once someone has accepted that they are not monoamorous, they will have no choice but to step out. Even with the lifejacket of knowing one can always move back to monoamory, the ocean of polyamory can feel scary. And faking monoamory is not hard—many do it for years. Whether these lives are happy, content, or enriched, depends on what people aim to achieve with them.

The first stage of coming out comprises accepting being polyamorous. There is a difference between just falling in love with more than one person and deciding to lead a polyamorous life. I know some people who understand that they have polyamorous tendencies but have chosen to remain committed to just one partner because they see that as a more peaceful and hassle-free life choice. This is different from faking monoamory. Here, people are not in denial; they accept they are polyamorous, yet choose to remain monoamorous, thus placing their other desires on hold consciously and carefully. I have seen this work better when one does this for oneself rather than justifying it for a partner. In the latter case, there may be a latent grudge that grows out of a sense of having sacrificed something precious for the partner. If the partner is not 'grateful' enough, this grudge can take ungainly turns. But after accepting that one is polyamorous, if one decides to follow the path of living that life, then it requires further consideration. It is not just important to understand one's desires but also to ask if one is willing to go on this difficult journey where everything we have known and accepted about love and relationships may be questioned and reinterpreted.

The second stage is the actual coming out, if one so desires. This needs to be planned in phases with help from trusted friends or people from the community. This may include coming out to parents, larger families, friends, or the public in general. Many of us first come out in support groups. However, the hardest coming out happens among partners or spouses when a person decides to lead a polyamorous life after years in monoamory. It is always better to begin with conversations in a safe and respectful environment because the reactions of those at the receiving end can be hurtful, angry, and sometimes even violent. One has to decide the pace and timing of the coming out according to the context, and not give in to any kind of pressure from anyone. One of the many fears that I see people in our community live with is over being outed by someone else before one is prepared. This causes a lot of damage and we must be very careful. In this part of the journey, the community plays a crucial role of providing support.

One would think that life gets easier once 'out'. Unfortunately, that's when the struggle of facing the music from society begins. The judgements start pouring in, as do hate and ridicule. It is more bearable if one can find support groups in the cities where we live so that there are some safe places. There are also those who believe that it is best not to publicly come out but just be out to friends, family if they are open minded, and within dating paradigms. This is a more practical way and is considered safer.

THE PRICE

It hasn't been easy for me to live as a polyamorous woman. But then, when has love ever been painless—mono, triangular, or poly? To those who keep asking me whether I miss the supposed insurance of a single partner and their exclusive loyalty, on good days I say that the premium seems too high for me; and on bad days I remind them of the disloyal discovered late and the dead gone early, taking with them their promises of undying togetherness.

But is there a price to be paid for all our loves? Mimi, a dear friend who is monoamorous, often discusses with me the different prices we pay for our choices. She feels that her life, seen as more stable, and mine, seen as more free, are equally difficult and enriching. When I share the price I pay for my choice of being polyamorous, she reminds me of the price she pays to live within conventions. This latter is a price that is not accounted for because it has become invisible to us over time. If we did acknowledge it, we would perhaps realize how high it is, especially for women and other marginalized genders and sexualities. It becomes pointless to compare which price is higher. It suffices to say that polyamory, with all its difficulties, offers the possibility of a life where we do not have to lie about our desires in order to save ourselves or others.

9

THE GREEN FLAGS : WHEN TO
POLYAM AND HOW

Ma loves the Hindi film *Rajnigandha* (1974) and anytime it is telecast, she sits right there in front of the TV. I would sit around her too, and have watched the film several times. But it wasn't until much later, when Aditya, one of my partners, pointed it out, that I noted the beautiful lyrics of one of the songs. It said, 'Kayi baar yun bhi dekha hai, ye jo mann ki seema rekha hai, mann todne lagta hai, anjani pyaas ke peechhe, anjani aas ke peechhe, mann daudne lagta hai.' Written by Yogesh, composed by Salil Choudhary, and sung by Mukesh, this song says, 'I have seen this many times, this boundary that is drawn around the heart—the heart breaks it, and chases unknown longings and aspirations.' In the film, this is when the heroine is developing feelings for someone other than her partner. In the same song, she asks later, 'Kis ko meet banaoon, kis kee preet bhulaoon (Whom shall I consider a lover, whose love shall I attempt to forget)'?

I have found this a key question that initiated many of our polyamorous lives. Because we did not wish to grieve the loss of either of our loves and wanted to savour the joys of both. Because we did not want to make this decision a mandatory aspect of being in love. But most of all, because we felt we had the strength and expansiveness of heart to love both, and more.

GETTING STARTED

There are those who realize they are polyamorous, practise it quietly at first and then want to come out to their loved ones and the general public. This process has various stages that I have discussed in detail in the previous chapter. However, sometimes, people who have been monoamorous or monogamous for some time may decide to explore being polyamorous—alone or with their partners. This journey may be catalysed by their own intellectual queries about monoamory or more practically, from an experience of being strongly attracted to someone or falling in love again while already being in a deeply committed relationship. They would be wondering like the protagonist of the film *Rajanigandha*, 'Whom shall I consider a lover; whose love shall I attempt to forget?' It is not easy to throw away the principles of monoamory that are intertwined with our lives and psyche. But for those brave-hearts who would still like to embark on this road, there are a few steps to consider.

The first is to understand who will participate in this quest. For people who are single, this is easy. For those who are in dedicated partnerships or are married, this would mean finding out if their partner, too, wants to be a co-traveller. Sometimes, couples take this plunge together and that is often the best way forward. But if one partner wants to explore and the other does not, it is hard for both. The one who does not want to explore feels betrayal, wonders what they did wrong or what went amiss in their relationship, and is in anger and pain. The one who wants to explore feels anxiety, guilt, and shame. Especially in relationships that have been stable and kind, where partners have been deeply in love with each other for many years, this can come as a rude shock. However, the best thing to do is to allow for conversations over a period of time before taking any action. These talks can help both partners see a future beyond the haze of the present— one that they may both like to pursue. This future would not look like the one that they imagined at the beginning of their relationship, but it would certainly accommodate some aspects of both their desires. However, if this meeting point is not possible, then one partner must either step out of the relationship or accept the other's will. As discussed in the chapter about difficulties of polyamorous lives, a relationship between a monoamorous and a polyamorous person can be severely contentious. It is important to realize that while it may seem that one partner is suffering more in this situation, in reality, both have a difficult time navigating this.

The next step is to ask what prompted this need to explore and how important those prompts are in their lives. For couples, prompts can come from the boredom of being together for a long time, the slow erosion of a sense of meaning and value in the togetherness of life, or simply the curiosity to discover other worlds of romance, sex, and love. Some couples have deeper philosophical and political critiques of monoamory and question if the confines of it are stunting their growth individually and together. There is also the situation where one of the partners falls in love with someone and realizes that they would not like to just 'move on' to the next relationship or 'lose' that to remain in the current one. They would like a third option. That third option is opening their monoamorous lives to a different set of possibilities.

While single people may also feel some of these prompts, for them, there is another prompt which is important. The stress and anxiety of dating in today's competitive world in search for 'the one' only to be disillusioned time and again, create a distaste for monoamory. This also leads to polyamory. While contemplating on these reasons, people should really ask the tough question: are these reasons strong enough to sustain the difficult journey into polyamory? One can always come back to monoamory later, but it would be unfortunate if that return is full of regrets. Therefore, it is good to ask all the knockout questions right at the beginning, even if answers are unavailable at that moment.

Once the decision to take the plunge is made, it is time to think through what kind of relationships the people involved would like to explore individually or together. There are different ways of pushing the boundaries of monogamy or monoamory. This includes open relationships where only sexual relationships are engaged in, swinging among couples where partners are exchanged, engaging in group sex where partners share each other, or the full sway of polyamory where one is looking at building long-term relationships of love with more than one person.

Here one could use the practical exercise that I learnt from a wise polyamorous friend. People could make three lists for their new journey: the first of everything they would certainly like to do or try; the second of everything they certainly will not do or try; and the third of areas that they are still thinking about. This helps individuals understand their self-suggested boundaries, and still leaves enough room for play. For couples, it is important, at this stage, to have clarity about each other's limits. They may also realize that their need and appetite for risk are at different levels. It is vital to come to terms with what will be acceptable to both. This part needs to be built on absolute honesty even if the revelations of desire cause discomfort to a partner for the time being. Any deceit or even nondisclosures here come back to haunt couples later in their journey. These are difficult conversations for people who have lived monoamorous lives for a long time, so one has to be patient.

A friend once jokingly told me that it would be amazing to try out non-monoamory if only there was a map to guide us. While everyone's journey is different, there are resources online, books, articles, and interviews that one can read to understand more about the diverse ways in which one can explore beyond monoamory. If one can, speaking to travellers who have already embarked on this path is also a good idea to comprehend the joys and challenges that come with these practices.

In most cases, the journey starts with opening up the relationship to sexual encounters first, since sexual jealousy often seems to be the biggest hurdle for people to cross before they can think of sharing bonds of love. Having said that, each person or couple has a unique trajectory of their own adventure. Some go back to monoamory after a while, some remain flirting with non-monoamory involving open relationships and multiple casual sexual relationships, while others move on to polyamory. These shifts are neither binary nor linear and there can be infinite ways in which this exploration pans out.

- If you find yourself in a polyamorous situation without intending to, then the very first step is that you determine whether you want to explore this way of life or not. There will be gains and losses on both sides—evaluate them as much as you can and decide. If you intend to go ahead, the rest of the tips are the same for you as for those who choose to explore this way of being with full intention. If not, then you must walk out of whatever you have been thrown into. No matter how difficult that might be.

- For those who purposefully want to explore the polyamorous way of life—begin at the beginning. Join a few dating apps after verifying their credibility. Mention the kind of relationships that you are looking for. The apps today also give various options to describe what kind of relationship you are already in. Choose the one closest to where you think you are in your relationship status. This can signal your needs for exploration.

- Take it slow, take it easy.

- Trust your instincts—don't listen to those who coerce or attempt to influence you into doing what you don't feel well about or ready to do.

- Be honest, expect honesty. Do not compromise here.

- These new roads are less travelled—there will be wrong turns. That's okay. Most mistakes are learning experiences.

- If you are a couple exploring this, keep talking to each other. Try not only to be supportive of the experiments, but also to forgive the failures.

- If you are hurt, take time to heal. Don't rush.

- If you hurt another, apologize. Be there as they heal. Don't rush.

- Be slow to respond to online advances. Start conversations at a gentle pace. Take time to think through responses.

- Find at least one friend whom you can trust with this experiment—someone who will not hesitate to speak the truth when they think you have messed up. Someone who will still support you when you have messed up. Someone you don't have to agree with about you having messed up and they will still remain truthful.

- Don't expect too many friends to understand this. Even if they love you a lot.
- Keep a diary or notes of the journey—this helps later to access how far we have come from the starting point if we have to ever evaluate our life's journeys.
- Develop a radar to detect predators, bullies, bullshit, and bullshitters. Like every world, this one has its own set of miscreants. Safety must come before everything else.

While these are some tips that will help with the beginning of the journey, there are two important things one must never forget. Firstly, deciding to explore polyamory does not mean that one must immediately come out. One has responsibility to be honest with the self and the partner, if any. No one else needs to know. One can come out to others if, as, and when one is ready. Secondly, this is not a journey from where there is no turning back. One can decide to quit, go back to monoamory, remain undecided, or decide on any other path at any time. Again, the primary responsibilities lie with oneself and partners, if any. Explanations, apologies, or farewells need only be addressed to them.

BEING PARENTS OF THE EXPERIMENTAL YOUNG

After I started writing about polyamory, there were concerns brought to me by several women in their forties and fifties who are mothers of young adults, with middle-class, urban, educated backgrounds. People in their late teens and twenties today are experimenting with various kinds of sexualities, gender identities, and relationship structures while they are still in school and college. Polyamory is among the various explorations they are engaged in. For the parents—even those who are liberal in their values— these are uncharted territories. Their own worlds have remained primarily monogamous and cis-heterosexual. Very few of them have any friends outside of these boundaries. Most of them do not have the wherewithal to enter the worlds of their children.

Even those who try to read up online, find themselves completely at sea without anyone to guide them. Filled with grave concern and anxiety about their children, they are unable to share these worries with their family members or friends for the fear of their children being judged.

Some of these parents shared with me that young people at this age do not really understand the consequences of the choices they are making. 'Playing with fire, they are,' said someone whose daughter refuses to come home too often from the hostel. Some even believe that, because in some campuses and peer groups it is 'trendy' to be queer or polyamorous, there is peer pressure, bullying, and coercion. They feel that in this unhealthy high-pressure lifestyle of being different and having many lovers, what matters is keeping score and scoring high, not developing nurturing bonds. One mother explained this to me using pornography as reference. She said that while adults choosing to watch pornography are generally making informed decisions, children watching it might develop highly distorted ideas of sexual intimacy. Similarly, what is often practised in the name of polyamory among young people are half-baked and misunderstood ways of having multiple, indiscriminate sexual partners, she said. This could give young people an anamorphic view of love, she worried.

THE WORKSHOPS OF THE YOUNG

Given how serious the issue is, I decided to spend some time with young adults in their late teens and twenties, attempting to understand their quest for life. What I saw among most of them was a strong interrogation of conventional lives lived by their parents and expected from them.

Kabir is in his twenties, in college, and identifies as a trans-masc, non-binary, queer person. He questions the status quo and norms of society and attempts to live a life that feels honest and true to him. For him, exploring non-monogamy through polyamory is critical to expressing himself. He said, 'For a heart that can never run out of love to share, being polyamorous means living life authentically and with an evergreen curiosity. It makes me practise healthy habits like introspecting, grounding, being honest, and being communicative. It lets me express my care, love, and passion in safe ways. And it allows me to experience every person and every relationship as new and different. This not only helps me build multiple support systems, but also maintains my own individuality and sufficiency.'

For Madham (name chosen), in their twenties, also in college, who identifies as a gender-fluid, queer, and polyamorous person, love and intimacy were always meant to be shared with multiple partners. They were unfamiliar with terms like 'polyamory' growing up, but when they did find these terms, they 'connected with the concept immediately and without insecurity'. Since they had already explored their gender and sexuality from a very young age and realized they were queer, discovering being polyamorous did not worry them at all. They had 'learnt to ignore the norms'.

For Brijesh (name changed), also in their twenties and identifying as a trans-fem, non-binary, queer person, being polyamorous is part of exploring the various contours of gender, sexuality, and relationships. They shared, 'For me, being polyamorous is an active choice. It is a way of living that mirrors values such as freedom and honesty. I just don't get the concept of controlling someone else's expectations. Exclusivity is a construct of capitalist romance, and love, in its true form, is about liberation from such views.' They added, 'It's about recognizing that care, compassion, and connection don't have to be limited to one person or one kind of relationship.... I do believe that love, in all its forms, can be a very powerful tool in creating a more empathetic and more relatable world.' They feel that polyamory is more than simply a question of romantic relationship status; it is a way of building community through giving and receiving love and support.

What I noticed in my conversations with many of these young people was their desire to remain 'fluid' in how they want to define themselves with respect to not just their relationships of love and intimacy but also their gender and sexuality. This fluidity is what enabled them to explore, experiment, learn, change, or embrace as they go along. For Brijesh, this journey is 'a place of...confusion and acceptance'. Even when they know they don't have the answers, they are 'learning to embrace the unknown and to trust in the journey, knowing it's valid even if it doesn't look like anyone else's'. Kalpi (name changed), who thinks she may like 'boys more than girls' but does not want to 'freeze it yet', has dropped out of college to work for a sports company. She is exploring being polyamorous. She feels that her feud was with the 'fixity of everything at birth'. She said, 'From caste to character, everything is finalized at birth, giving me no choice to become who I want to.' Being 'fluid helps to flow underneath those barriers' for Kalpi.

Many of these young people started their journeys early, in school, through conversations with friends, engaging with online communities to explore their questions, and reading up. They are aware; they read and they search for communities of like-minded people, especially when they don't receive understanding or support from their homes. Brijesh mentioned, 'This community that I found along the way has been a big source of my strength. And I feel really lucky to have been able to connect with people who are like, "Oh, I know what it's like to change genders. I know what it's like to be gay. I know what it is like to be in alternative or non-traditional relationships."' They added that, 'Knowing that there are others out there who have fought and are still fighting battles for our rights, gives me the courage to keep going.' Some of them are also dealing with difficulties within the community. Madham was concerned that their ideal definition of polyamory—that of committed exclusivity within a closed group, understood as polyfidelity—may never be realized since most people they meet want open relationships. I also noticed that while many of the young people I spoke to engage in casual sexual relationships, they are more discerning when it comes to love.

I don't have children of my own, but if I did, they would be the age of these young people. I asked them what their expectations were from us, the generation of their parents, both from within the community of queer and polyamorous people as well as those outside of it. Kabir said, 'For people within the community...I have sincere gratitude for the lives they have lived and shared with us. The only thing I can ask of them is to keep their minds, hearts, and homes open to all who dare to question the norm and resist them. Their guidance is crucial, and so is their resistance.' Brijesh sums up with clear expectations: 'I really feel that what I would want to see from your generation is sensitivity and understanding, both within our community and outside of it. I mean, I truly understand that things are moving really fast, and concepts regarding gender, sexuality, and relationships today may stand poles apart from what one grew up with. But what I hope is that, though probably new and a little awkward at first, you come to it with an open mind, ready to learn, to listen.' Madham shared, 'Work with us, teach us, pass the baton to us, and help us understand each other's perspectives. We too have ideas and aspirations for the community, which can only be achieved if we have your support and your experience to guide us. And do use the knowledge, privilege, and platform you may have to advocate for legal protections and social support systems for people, younger and older alike.'

What was difficult to hear was that most people I met had no expectations from their own parents who, they thought, did not understand them. Sometimes, they felt let down and at others, they just didn't want to have anything to do with them. While Kalpi mentioned that she would like her family to understand her choices, she did not think that would ever happen. Madham said, 'I cannot dream in a thousand years about coming out to them—the most I might share is liking girls. My gender-fluidity and polyamory will always stay hidden from them.... This detachment has been the case for a long while now and I don't see my family life as providing the context to any part of my queer identity.'

What was very heartening for me to see was that amidst their various challenges, they make courageous and sincere attempts to push boundaries of imagination. Many of them are creative, articulate, and have deep compassion for each other. They are also thinking of community-building and social justice for various kinds of marginalized and vulnerable people of society. Amidst all of this, they are experimenting with life. I developed deep respect for those I listened to.

GETTING STARTED AS PARENTS OF THE EXPERIMENTAL YOUNG

Not being a parent, I do not presume to give any advice to those who are struggling with this young and experimental generation. However, since some parents have had conversations with me and asked me questions, I would like to respond to their anxieties, informed by the insights I have gained from my engagement with the young people. It is very important for parents to take these questions, investigations, and choices of their children seriously. The fact that some of these choices may shift and change in the future is no reason to underestimate them as either casual or fleeting. It will help tremendously if parents read and understand about the complexities of gender, sexualities, and various kinds of love and relationships. They may find it useful to introspect and see what kind of prejudices and biases they have. They may discover that what they recognize as 'worry' for their children actually comes from their own fear of the unknown. In the process, parents may realize that, in many cases, a part of their children's need to question and challenge norms comes from judging, albeit harshly sometimes, the lives of the parents which they view as being glued together with many silences and some denials.

My suggestion is that instead of pushing monoamory as the only way upon their children, they could have a conversation with them about the different options one has in terms of love and relationships. They will need to be open to learn about their children, from their children. But they must also accept that as is the case world over in every generation, young people will most certainly continue to experiment, with or without engaging in discussions with their parents. All we can hope for is that if they need us at any time, we are there to support them; and even if slightly singed from these laboratory tests, they will emerge more knowledgeable, not too damaged, and joyfully ready to embrace life in all its diverse complexities.

10

THE RED FLAGS: WHEN NOT
TO POLYAM AND WHY

When I was thinking of making this book, I knew that there had to be a chapter on red flags. This is because, from the time I started sharing my experiences of polyamory in the public domain, many people, mostly heterosexual women (but not just them), connected with me privately to share stories that were disconcerting. While some raised concerns about dodgy definitions of polyamory commonly touted by men, others had disturbing narratives of outright abuse through manipulation, coercion, and deception, mostly by heterosexual cis-gender men, all in the name of polyamory. The women sometimes sought my advice or opinion, and sometimes told me sharply that this whole world of polyamory was a sham, a facade for preying on vulnerable people.

Harsh as it may have sounded to me, someone who struggled hard to live ethically with polyamory, I understood where they came from and why the hurt and anger were so deep. In their experiences, they were stripped of their dignity and their sense of self, which impacted their confidence, ability to take risks, and their capacity for hope. This chapter is inspired by their struggle to heal, and is my effort to acknowledge their pain. I am sharing some of the stories and my reading of them within the context of considering or practising polyamory. While in most cases, I have listened to one side of the incidents, I do have a sharp ear for knowing truth when it is told. For the sake of confidentiality and comprehension, I have used fictional names, and gleaned the issues from the various stories shared with me to reconstruct them, highlighting the key problem areas.

FOUR STORIES

Let's say her name is Nisha and his, Sameer. They were seeing each other for a few months. After the first few dates, they became sexually intimate and soon stopped dating others to become exclusive lovers. Or so Nisha was told. After a few months, Nisha brought up moving in together but Sameer did not respond. One day Nisha caught him, doing what she understood as 'cheating'. He said that he was polyamorous and would like her to open up to the idea as well. This was the first time Nisha was hearing about this from Sameer, so she felt both unprepared and startled. She asked for some time to think about it. Since that day, Sameer kept forcing the idea on Nisha, openly criticizing her inability to see their relationship in a 'progressive' light. He went on to raise doubts about her feminism, saying that to be truly sexually free as a feminist, she needed to embrace polyamory. Nisha was confused. While she was not wholly against attempting to understand and try out the idea, Sameer's incessant coercion and provocations made her feel vulnerable and miserable.

In the second story, Jane and Amit were a monoamorous couple well into their fourth year of a live-in relationship. Suddenly, one day, Amit expressed the desire to introduce a new person into their sex life, a close male friend of his. In response to Jane's bewilderment, he said that he wanted to try out polyamory and desired to introduce Jane to the idea. When Jane refused to participate, he rebuked her and questioned the integrity of her love for him. When she proposed to seek counselling together to understand the situation better, he completely disengaged and gave her the ultimatum that either she agreed to turn polyamorous or this would be the end of their relationship. Jane felt angry and slightly lost.

In the third story, when Alok and Saba started seeing each other, Alok clearly told Saba that he was polyamorous. Saba shared that she was not. However, both had fallen deeply in love with each other, so they decided to see where this would go, with Alok continuing to date others while Saba remained monoamorous.

Soon, what started to bother Saba was that Alok would share with her the details of each of his other relationships. She specifically told him that these stories affected her mental balance. She was walking a tightrope with his polyamorous life and the stories triggered her insecurities, making her feel extremely vulnerable. Alok insisted that this was the only way for such a relationship to work and continued to share the stories. Saba suspected that in a sadistic way, he relished the anxiety she went through while listening. He neither helped her decode these relationships, nor worked out ways of moving past her discomfort. Saba felt helpless and heartbroken.

In the fourth story, Ravi and Natasha knew they were both polyamorous when they started their relationship. In fact, they were very happy to have found each other, given the stigma around polyamorous identities. They agreed to be each other's primary partner. But soon, Natasha noticed that the number of Ravi's 'partners' galloped at an accelerated rate. There would be several new additions in a few months and the older ones would disappear without much mention. Though they had both agreed to share their relationships with each other, in time, Ravi's sharing reduced steadily. All this happened without much conversation with her. Every time Natasha tried to sit with Ravi to frame some rules and boundaries within the polyamorous framework, Ravi avoided it, leaving Natasha wondering about the ethics of his polyamory. She also felt betrayed over not being part of the journey when they had decided that they would be primary partners for each other.

REVIEW

These stories came to me with an entanglement of questions, bewilderment, pent-up anger, and grief. There were unresolved feelings of being abandoned and betrayed, grave doubts about the self, and distrust of others. As I closely analysed each case, I noticed common red flags.

In the first story, Sameer decided to tell Nisha that he was polyamorous only when he was caught cheating. This is always a fluttering red flag. Without any judgement about casual sex, one must understand that polyamory is not about having sex with more than one person. Hiding behind this definition does a disservice to those who are struggling to lead ethical polyamorous lives. The confession also came after Nisha and Sameer decided to see each other exclusively. One would think that if Sameer was polyamorous, he would have brought it up before such a decision was taken. However, even if we give Sameer the benefit of the doubt with respect to the timing of his confession, considering the difficulties polyamorous people go through coming out, what happened next begs no excuse. He did not prepare Nisha for this sharing, was not ready to give her time to think for herself as to how she felt, and kept pressurizing her to accept polyamory as a way of life when she was confused. These are not just signs of an uncaring bully, they are also the markers of a man simply caught out cheating and retro-justifying his actions. However, the most exploitative part of this was his questioning her feminism on account of her refusal to accept polyamory. I have heard this absolutely bunkum provocation in many stories that were shared with me. It is important to make it very clear that while feminism means different things to different people and manifests in diverse social and political ways, of which polyamory may be one, being polyamorous is certainly not a prerequisite to being a feminist. Also, being polyamorous is not a more or less progressive way of living than monoamory. It is just another, albeit different, way of loving. For anyone to use feminism or progressive politics as rationalizations to force their partners into polyamory is abuse.

The second story pans out much like the first one in its suddenness, pressure, and rebuke, except here Jane thought she knew Amit well in the four years that they had been together. The fact that he wanted to change his way of loving without a conversation with her, and in addition, came to her with a proposal for a friend to join them, threw Jane off completely. This was a destruction of trust. Jane felt further let down when Amit put up a wall and refused to engage. Amit was keeping all the cards to himself and controlling the relationship without any consultation with Jane.

His passive aggression left Jane with an 'either fall in line, or quit' ultimatum. This type of coercion with emotional tyranny, especially when it comes with questioning a person's sincerity in love, is both manipulative and abusive. In this case, with the involvement of a friend—a third person—Jane felt even more exposed and vulnerable. Across all of polyamory's various ways of being, there is never any compromise on a person's dignity and self-worth. And that's exactly what Amit had put at stake here with Jane.

The third story is a difficult one because of the involvement of a polyamorous and a monoamorous person. I have discussed the various complications in the nature and practice of such a relationship in the chapter dealing with challenges of a polyamorous life. So, without getting into those details again, here I will concentrate on the specific way in which the polyamorous person behaved and the problems that arise from it. Alok's insistence on sharing stories of his other lovers with Saba, which she had requested him to refrain from, is cruel. Even in relationships where both partners are polyamorous, there is always a carefully thought through and mutually agreed upon understanding on the limits of sharing. Alok not only shared what Saba was uncomfortable with, he also decided the terms of engagement of the relationship on his own without any consultation with Saba. This made Saba anxious and unhappy. She kept feeling inferior to Alok as he continued with his annals of many desires. This kind of abuse can be severely damaging to a person's confidence and self-worth.

In the fourth story, Natasha is right to question Ravi's claim of being a polyamorous person. In light of the speed with which his constellation of partners kept changing, it would be fair to wonder whether these were casual relationships of sex and not really polyamory. Polyamory is embedded with a desire to build relationships. In Ravi's case, it was hard to see the intention of that commitment. The terms of their relationship were forged on the foundation of both being polyamorous, where each had the freedom to engage in other relationships but not just casual sexual encounters. Therefore, even if Amit wanted this, he needed to first revisit the initial terms and come to a consensual agreement with

Natasha. The second understanding in their relationship was that they would share with each other about their new partners so that they felt included in each other's lives as primary partners. That rule, too, was being flouted. In any polyamorous relationship, while the idea is to be open to more than one relationship, if the numbers start multiplying rapidly, suddenly, and without much dialogue with the primary partner, then it is time for a conversation.

Listening to these various stories, I have realized that one must be careful when engaging in polyamory or opening up relationships with polyamorous people. This warning is especially relevant for women, queer people, those already marginalized by caste, race, ability, religion, and more, because it is easy to take advantage of them amidst the unequal power balances of the world they inhabit. They get ensnared in apparently progressive relationships, which are nothing but traps. The survivors are left in various states of injury, struggling to heal. This is particularly rough because they also feel, even if subconsciously, that in some way, this is their punishment for straying from the good and narrow path of righteous monoamory.

Love is often an easy tool for manipulation. While those who fake polyamory abuse people, within the networks of practising polyamorous people, too, there are predators. They use love for self-aggrandizement and self-centred gratifications. They could be collectors, score-keepers in competition with each other, toxic hierarchy-setters, or simply addicted to the adrenaline that comes with the rush of being desired by many.

THE RED FLAGS

To summarize, some of the red flags that one could look out for in relationships where polyamory plays a role are as follows:

- Polyamory is spoken of only in terms of multiple sexual relationships and not as a way of building relationships.
- There is no clarity in what is being proposed, its terms and conditions, and how it will impact the partners. It is altogether hazy or convoluted or both.

- Rules mutually agreed upon are repeatedly flouted without consulting partners.
- There is no honest sharing of the past or current situations even when sharing has been agreed upon.
- There is no time or effort spent in preparing the partner for changes or re-prioritization, or introduction of any new element in the relationship.
- There is only one-way communication and the partner is not heard.
- The partner's fear and anxiety are not given importance. In fact, in some cases, they are ridiculed as regressive.
- There is no attempt to understand the need to bring in help from the outside if required, in the form of a friend or a counsellor.
- There is no active process of building mutual consent.
- In the case of a relationship between a monoamorous and a polyamorous person, there is pressure put on the partner to accept polyamory as a way of life for themselves as well.
- Polyamory is touted as a more progressive, more feminist, or more politically radical and freer way of life and loving while denigrating other ways of being.

While these red flags have always acted as precautions for people, the suggestion here is to first determine how much one would like to risk for a relationship and then decide what to do with the particular red flag one has encountered. Each one of us has a different appetite for risk, gamble, and trouble. We also have wildly diverse views on what is safe and dangerous as far as love is concerned. One must act according to one's own analysis of the situation and ability to persevere while keeping the consequences of the red flags in mind. Finally, and this I cannot emphasize enough, no one must ever be in a relationship they do not want, and where they do not fully consent to not just the nature of the relationship, but also its terms, conditions, and responsibilities. Even if hesitant and not loudly spoken—a no always means a no. Anyone saying anything otherwise is suspect.

11

BOAT OF HOPE III
'THE BULWARK OF LOVE IS ENOUGH
TO GET US THROUGH'

Lea Christen is an educator who teaches children in a primary school in Zurich. She is also a sexual health worker and counsellor, teaching children and counselling parents about sexual health issues. She is in her thirties. Kaushik Bhaduri is an IT professional who lives and works in Kolkata. He is in his early fifties. They use she/her and he/him as their pronouns respectively. They have been in a relationship for seven years now and both are polyamorous. While they live in separate continents, their relationship has grown over spending months with each other in India and Switzerland, travelling together, and mail and video calls for the rest of the time. Kaushik started his journey with polyamory in his twenties. Lea practised open sexual relationships initially and then moved on to explore polyamory in the past few years. Though they remain passionately polyamorous in spirit and philosophy, currently, they do not have any partners other than each other. I have known them as my chosen family for a long time, and had the pleasure of a conversation on their journey of polyamory with all its joys and struggles. Here are excerpts that take us through some of their ideas, practices, and concerns as polyamorous people.

(A. G.: Arundhati Ghosh / L. C.: Lea Christen / K. B.: Kaushik Bhaduri)

ON DISCOVERING POLYAMORY

A. G.: Lea, how did you discover polyamory?

L. C.: It was more of a process for me. My initial relationships, starting when I was a teenager, were all monoamorous. I was socialized into it and didn't know any other way to be. I also thought that my (then) boyfriend and I would be together forever. And then, in my early twenties, I started to experiment with open relationships. I questioned if one person could fulfil all my needs. It was more about sexual fulfilment then. So, my partner and I opened up to other sexual relationships but we never really fell in love with anyone. The talk about polyamory never occurred because nobody came up in our lives.

But then I met Kaushik in 2015, when I was travelling in India. He and I got to know each other. I was still seeing my boyfriend back home—for about three years then. I started to develop strong feelings for Kaushik. When I came home, I started to think about it—I realized that I had feelings for two men. I started to research it, read books, and also spoke to people. I also talked a lot with Kaushik about it, because when I met Kaushik, he was already telling me about polyamory. So, I also think Kaushik taught me a few things there. This was just the beginning. Then I started to process how I wanted to be polyamorous and how to handle the situation that I had someone I loved in Switzerland and another in India. I started asking, what does this mean for me? What does this mean for my life? That was the beginning.

A. G.: *The same question goes to you Kaushik—how did you discover polyamory?*

K. B.: You have known me for a very long time. You know I come from a relatively liberal family. I had access to free interaction with the other gender, unlike what happened in many other families when we were growing up. But polyamory was not in any conscious paradigm for me then. But in my mid-twenties, I went to the United States. I had a housemate who was the local pastor of a pagan community. It was through her that I got a window into a certain lifestyle, a living philosophy that included polyamory. I was a part of that community for some time because I resonated with the beliefs. At the same time, I read *The Ethical Slut, Sex at Dawn*, and *The story of O*—they all expanded my sexual horizon and understanding of myself. This carried on for some time but I got detached from that community fairly soon because I realized it also came with a lot of rituals and other stuff that I wasn't so much into. But the idea of polyamory and the idea of non-monogamous love within an ethical paradigm are things that I carried forward in my heart from then on.

ON BEING POLYAMOROUS

A. G.: So where are you with polyamory today in your life?

L. C.: It's interesting. After seeing both Kaushik and my other partners for three years, I decided to come to India to live here for some time. I split up with my former boyfriend because I didn't know how long I would stay in India. Since then, I have gone back and forth between India and Switzerland and been with Kaushik but I haven't had deep feelings for anybody else which could grow into another relationship. Today, my attitude towards love and philosophy is polyamorous but I do not have any partner other than Kaushik.

A. G.: Why do you think that is? Was it a decision or just perchance?

L. C.: Kaushik and I have tried to discuss the reasons and I have some insights into this now. I think this pause has happened due to various reasons. This long-term and long-distance relationship needs a lot of energy and time. While he and I have a lot of discussions, I feel that him being so far away from me physically is hard. If he were to meet someone else and have a relationship, it would just explode, in the current moment. It would just be too much. We are still figuring this out, asking what our future looks like—being in separate countries, so far away. I think while I am philosophically always open to new people, right now, I have no space to meet someone new or start another relationship.

A. G.: Kaushik, where do you stand with this?

K. B.: I'm on lockstep with what Lea said. It wasn't like a decision we took consciously to be exclusive, but that's what has happened for now. If you ask me about our journey—this is what I will say. First, it was falling in love, then it was figuring out what this sort of polyamorous situation means, and then figuring out all the troubles of a long-distance relationship. After eight years now, I think this is a phase where we are trying to understand further about where we would go from here. We know that this is the primary partnership around which other things can happen, but we are in the consolidation phase of that primary first.

But I have no doubt, and Lea, too, feels the same, that we are polyamorous and will be open for other people. I think we both know it and it would not shock us if the other person falls in love or in some way, has a romantic connection with another person. We will need a great deal of conversation, communication, and reorganizing perhaps, but I think we are fundamentally people who genuinely believe that it can happen when the time comes for it.

ON REDEFINING LOVE

A. G.: Lea, when you say you are currently not pursuing a polyamorous relationship, or practising it, does it mainly mean the sexual and romantic context only, or are there other emotional dimensions?

L. C.: If you ask me about love, I will say I am practising polyamory in many other ways than just sexual and romantic. I feel so much affection for a lot of different people with whom I am not romantically or sexually involved. I also don't create any hierarchy between friendships and romantic relationships. I share strong bonds with friends where I also feel physically close. For me, physical closeness is very important, sometimes more important than sexual closeness. From a very young age in my life, I had anxiety because I saw a lot of romantic relationships breaking up and a lot of women being alone because they had not nurtured friendships. I told myself this would not happen to me. It also lets me feel independent, free, and autonomous. That's why I like polyamory as a concept and stand behind it. I feel that I have a lot of love to give—different kinds of love and to different people, without creating a hierarchy.

A. G.: Kaushik, what do you think?

K. B.: I think I would go further than Lea in some ways. I would say, in my life, I have relationships where the love is palpable, and part of it is also tied to a sexuality that may have been once shared. It's not a context that is completely erased. It is an understanding that polyamory is not a licence for gay abandon but a responsible journey caring for all those who are part of it. So I'm just loving it and trying to adjust those barometers as I go along.

ON JEALOUSY

A. G.: Everybody asks polyamorous people, 'But what about jealousy?' So, what about jealousy?

L. C.: I feel jealousy often. With Kaushik being so far away, I'm jealous of all the people who can spend time with him because I can't do it. I feel they can have so much more time with him. I was also jealous when he dated other women. It is a very strong physical and emotional feeling. I had to understand it, rationalize it. By then, we had built up a lot of trust between us. I saw that he was also helping me. I sensed we were okay. I realized it was irrational to feel afraid of losing him, to feel I wasn't good enough. This helps me.

A. G.: Kaushik, how do you stand with jealousy?

K. B.: I want to give this answer in two parts. The first part is about me. I struggled a lot with jealousy. I believed that I could go through life like a bulletproof elephant, but it's not so. I keep realizing that in bits and pieces—especially for important people like you guys. I feel jealous and haven't mastered it. But I try very hard.

The second part is this story I want to share. Once, I was dating somebody and we went to have dinner with her best friend and her husband. This was the first time I was going to their house with my girlfriend. We knew that the husband was more conventional. We had dinner and then we all started drinking.

At one point, the husband went off to take a nap in the other room. My girlfriend, her friend, and I were in the living room. One thing led to another and we got really cosy. I mean a heavy necking kind of scenario. So, in the middle of all this, the guy comes out of the bedroom and sees us there—me, a complete stranger, cuddling with his wife. My first reaction was to bring him into the fold. So, I gave a very benign smile and indicated to him to join us—which he did. Now, what I did not know was that he already had the hots for my girlfriend, so, he was pretty happy about the situation. We passed out pretty quickly. And then the next morning, we woke up and left. This was never ever brought up. But the fun part is that later, after I got to know them a little bit better, at one time, this guy told me that this incident had actually changed his relationship with his wife. He used to be really jealous and would have these attacks of jealousy. But this incident helped him to work towards a much better relationship.

ON CO-LOVERS

A. G.: *What has been your relationship or attitude towards co-lovers of each other whom you've known?*

L. C.: I have met Sakina, Kaushik's erstwhile partner, and I feel very friendly with her. She has a history with Kaushik, dating long before we met. I feel very happy that she and Kaushik still feel so close to each other and trust each other. About the people Kaushik dated while we were together, I strongly wanted to know them. I'd ask Kaushik a lot of questions. However, I was not ready to meet them face to face. Felt a bit anxious. That would be the next level for me, but yes, I could have that one day.

A. G.: *Kaushik—what about co-lovers?*

K. B.: I tend to become best buddies with them. That's to do with the earlier partners or those you already know about when you enter a relationship. But I think it's more difficult if while she is with you, your partner gets involved with somebody else. Now, I have also been in that situation. In my experience, first, there is a lot of jealousy and this feeling of hollowness in the pit of your stomach. There is so much insecurity. But if there is enough meat in what I have with my partner, then definitely it has been possible for me to get over it. Once that initial angst is done with, I think a part of me switches on to taking that third person as an individual and not necessarily as somebody's lover. And we can bond.

ON TRUST, SECURITY, AND LOYALTY

A. G.: Now, I'll come to another aspect of relationships that monoamorous people swear by and wonder how polyamorous people work it out—trust, security, and loyalty. Easy definitions if you have just one partner, but what happens when you have multiple partners?

L. C.: I feel that when you have more than one partner and you want to be a good partner, you are forced to be even more aware of loyalty, security, and trust. These are the main pillars of any healthy relationship. You have to have deep and honest conversations about the relationship. You can't take anyone or any of the relationships for granted. You may build trust differently with different partners and define them. Polyamory opens up new conversations about these pillars.

A. G.: Kaushik, what do you think?

K. B.: People are very heteronormative and this debate does not go far with them. If people believe that loyalty means staying with one person in one sort of setup forever, then you can't fight that understanding. For me, it has been what I would call the 'love primary' paradigm. You really have to trust the love of the other person for you and the intent of that relationship, and the rest just flows. To me, trust, security, and loyalty are not even three different things. You just love and you value the love that the other person has for you—that is enough.

A. G.: So, how would the concept of trust be different?

K. B.: I've seen a sea captain, who has a very loving National

Park warden wife in a city. He goes to work on his ship for nine months every year. His wife has a much younger man as a lover and companion. All three of them are in this together. I don't know what security means to the man who is away at sea. But I imagine they have this worked out among them. That's the other thing. Polyamory is so different for different people.

L. C.: I thought a little bit about loyalty. Maybe it is even more important in polyamorous relationships than monoamorous ones, to follow commitments and obligations. It has to be taken seriously because one has to juggle different relationships. Because you have limited time with each partner, you have to listen deeply, be totally present for them in that situation. For those who just live with one partner full-time, it's different since you may have all the time.

ON DIFFICULTIES AND STRUGGLE

A. G.: What have been some of the difficult parts of your journey?

L. C.: I think having this long-distance relationship is the biggest difficulty. I cannot answer this separately from this aspect. We spend maybe four or five months together every year. While we communicate a lot on WhatsApp call, video, and we talk and narrate our everyday life, we lack experiencing life together. I have always struggled with this. Even when I had my other partner in Switzerland, the struggle of only listening to what they were doing with other people and not being able to actually participate or experience was tough.

A. G.: But wouldn't it be the same if Kaushik and you were monoamorous? How is it different, being polyamorous?

L. C.: It is more difficult. For example, if he is far away and has experiences with another partner, I have no way of meeting him later. The physical closeness, the body language, and being together give a lot of security to a relationship. It helps to know that it's okay, we are good. Sometimes, talking can be superficial, but being together physically makes so much more sense. That's why this huge continental distance is so difficult for me.

K. B.: I agree totally with Lea. I think this whole long-distance thing comes with its own set of problems. When two people are closer, the communication is of a completely different nature. In the absence of that, your mind just races. It creates more problems than there are. In modern times, when you're on something like a phone, for example, silence is way more silent. So, Lea and I struggled as openly polyamorous people, whether we had other people in our lives or not.

We also had our boundaries in terms of what we could expect from each other. Polyamory also comes with a degree of freedom to allow the other person enough space in figuring out what happens in their lives, how they want to see it, and what parts they want to share. All these things become much easier to handle if you're together in the same space and not thousands of miles away. It took a long time for us to come to a place where we have this deep sense of trust. We are still polyamorous people, and just that bulwark of love we have is enough to get us through.

L. C.: I think there are also some advantages to us being apart. We are more conscious about how to structure our lives and how to be with other loved ones. It doesn't have to be romantic or sexual. Maybe I feel more open about other relationships because Kaushik is not there. It also strengthens the philosophy that actually I have a big heart, I have an interest in other people, and I have space for them. That's why both of us have a lot of loved ones around us.

A. G.: *Kaushik, any examples you want to share from other relationships where you were polyamorous?*

K. B.: There's a difference between people figuring out that they are really polyamorous and wanting to match you step by step, and those who have felt they needed to be so because they wanted to be with you. I have had relationships with both (kinds of people). The second set of people soon find out that they can't handle polyamory. That becomes a very bitter journey. I've had situations where people have said, 'Hey, you bring a lot to the table and I love you a lot but I can't enjoy you in my life the way you are. I just get disbalanced with you in my life. So I just don't want to be near you.'

I've experienced heartaches and I've also experienced shortcomings in me. There are situations where you have set boundaries and know that you are allowed to get involved with others but being honest about it has an emotional cost that you don't want to bear. So you take the easy way out with a white lie. These are weaknesses I have experienced. One needs to know that nothing comes for free. There is always a cost to adopting a certain living philosophy.

A. G.: *How has coming out worked for you, Lea?*

L. C.: At the beginning of my journey, when I came out as polyamorous, my parents wrote it off as a phase. They thought I would outgrow it as I got older and wiser. They connected polyamory strongly with promiscuity and not being able to form meaningful relationships. I believe they felt anxious for me. But that's where the long journey with my parents started. Slowly, they started to understand what it meant for me. Being very close to me and knowing me well, they realized that it has nothing to do with being fickle or promiscuous. So, now, this is not even a topic of discussion with them anymore. They are able to witness from close, how polyamory is another way of building nurturing, strong, loving, and healthy relationships.

That's with my parents. But with others, I just tell them about polyamory when the context suits me. It takes time to be able to explain what this form of living entails for me. As it is also an intimate topic, I choose whom I share my stories with wisely. I don't want to waste my energy for minds that are set in stone. In the last decade, polyamory has become accepted in Central Europe. Many young people today choose this form of loving. I love this development because it means people have started to question the propagated 'almighty correct' heteronormative and monoamorous relationships.

A. G.: *Kaushik, what did people say when you came out?*

K. B.: That's a funny one. I have always been open about my polyamorous practices, so, I'm not sure if there was ever a 'coming out' moment. Some of the initial reactions I get, after the usual 'Poly what?' are, from men, 'So cool dude, but how do you manage?' or 'Gosh, isn't life complicated enough with just one girlfriend/ wife?' with some eye-rolling. I also hear, 'Where do you find such friends with benefits?' and 'Damn, it must be great to have threesomes all the time!' From women I hear, 'Oh that must mean you have seven girlfriends and they all let you cheat, ha ha!' By far, the most common one has been, 'I can't do all this nonsense. I am a jealous person.'

It's always funny to me that the perception of polyamory is as a license for promiscuity. For most people, there is not even a sliver of space for ethical and authentic human connection. As for reactions, how about asking, 'Are you happy being a polyamorous fella?' And if the answer is yes, then bloody end it by saying, 'Okay, then I'm happy too!'

ON BEING POLY

A. G.: What does it mean for you to be polyamorous?

L. C.: For me, the core of this lies in my attitude and philosophy on how to go through life, to practise and feel love, and my need to be in contact and connection with the people I love. As I said before, I do not believe in hierarchies. In societal terms, capitalism pushes us towards one monogamous heterosexual partnership. Society tells us what love is, how to love, how to proclaim love. Believing in polyamory helps me stay autonomous about my decisions on love. I do not rely on just one person but on the fact that there are several people in my life, and so is Kaushik.

K. B.: It was absolutely a defining moment of my life to have encountered polyamory and I embraced the basic principles of it. As far as human emotions and romantic love are concerned, polyamory is a lodestone, a kind of guiding map that I have. It has a very deep place in my heart. I don't know about anyone else, but that helped me out tremendously in my journey. I think it's a cornerstone of who I have become as a person ever since. So, that's just a personal aspect.

From a political perspective, I think it's a question of being in the minority. Today, many of us who are atheists or left–liberals find ourselves on the fringe of society. I have personally found myself to be a minority in many ways in this country in which I was born, as well as other parts of the world where I've travelled to. Being polyamorous is another aspect of being a minority. I have attempted to make other people understand atheism or dispel the myths around it. I am not sure I have been able to do anything about it. There are many such fundamental issues of our living. So, compared to those issues, polyamory is far away from common consciousness.

ON THE QUESTIONS THAT REMAIN

A. G.: What are some of the questions that remain for you in practising polyamory? Lea, what about you?

L. C.: I'm interested in how the whole movement of polyamory will develop. I am interested to see if it will have a bigger impact in society, be ingrained in law with protection of rights. At the moment, it's your parents, probably, and then your spouse who are legally responsible for you. They can decide on your behalf for your well-being if you are incapacitated or in hospital. So how will this change with polyamory? The same question comes up for children within polyamorous situations. If you have a child in a poly circle, how will parenting be freshly thought through? In a 'throuple', where there are three people in a relationship, can all three people be legal parents of a child? These are questions I think about.

A. G.: Kaushik, what are some of the questions that you continue to have about polyamory?

K. B.: One splinter thought, which is, what happens in the future when one relationship in a network of polyamory is one of these artificially intelligent companions? What are the legal ramifications if somebody, for example, leaves their money to this kind of entity? These will be relevant questions in the near future for sure. But for the current situation, I would say that the question of bandwidth is important. Whether it is due to professional commitments or societal and familial commitments, how much time can one give to building and nurturing relationships? There are so many things we like doing. So, how the concept of time management impacts polyamory is something I continue to enquire into.

ON CHANGING COURSE

A. G.: Lea, any doubts ever that made you think you should go monoamorous?

L. C.: No, I really don't think so. It's because you can be as polyamorous as you want to. You can define it as you want to. I don't have to have four different boyfriends all the time. I can be in different kinds of love. Knowing its bandwidth has helped me. I really feel everyone is polyamorous; they just have not explored it yet. Being polyamorous is not a risk for me—it is an advantage to be able to be free and autonomous in love.

A. G.: Any doubts, Kaushik, ever, that polyamory is not for you— that you should change?

K. B.: I have nothing to say but no, never.

12

BOAT OF HOPE IV
'THE INTOXICATION OF
FREEDOM IS ADDICTIVE'

Revathi (name changed) is a media professional. She is in her late
forties. Subir (name changed) is also a media professional and
married to Revathi. He is in his early fifties. They live together in
Mumbai. They use she/her and he/him pronouns respectively. Both
of them have been in sexual and romantic relationships with other
people while being married to each other. They have opened their
lives and hearts to many friends who have become lovers. I have
known them for a long time and when I asked them if they were
polyamorous, they first hesitated, and then said that they were not
sure. As we got talking, I realized that their sexual lives and ideas
of love are rich and multi-layered. While on some aspects, their
views differ from each other, they live with beauty, compassion,
and tenderness. They have created a polyamorous world of deep
friendships and trust. Unlike the earlier interviews, this one did
not keep to specific themes and was more free-flowing. Here is
the full conversation.

(A. G.: Arundhati Ghosh / R: Revathi / S: Subir)

*A. G.: What kind of relationships of love and sex do you have
outside of your marriage with Revathi?*
S: Revathi and I have been together since the time we were in
college some twenty-five years ago and we stumbled into the zone
of experimentation. My journey of experimentation started with her
and continues with her as the focal point of my life. It could be
that I never quite clicked so well and so securely with anyone else.

Over the years, while I have been married to Revathi, I have had relationships with some women friends. None of them were one-night stands. I deeply love all of them. Revathi and I have built friendships with them as well. Each of these relationships has been different for me and Revathi. They do not always need constant communication. For example, there is one woman whom I have not even met in many years. Sometimes, we connect through WhatsApp, but that, too, is rare. In fact, she is more in touch with Revathi than with me. But I still feel the same intensity towards her that I had felt when we started our relationship. We now live in different countries, but my sexual and romantic attraction to her remain the same. The connection is of a deeply trusting and very long friendship.

I feel the same way about another woman friend, who lives in a different city. We meet sometimes. She is married and has a child. We used to have a romantic and sexual relationship and still share a very tender and beautiful connection. I am not sure whether I can call it romantic now, and the sexual relationship has not been there for a very long time. But again, it's a very old friendship and camaraderie that Revathi and I share with her. After reading about polyamory, she said she was intrigued by the idea and felt close to it. She wanted to practise it. Perhaps she does in her own way. Her husband is a very nice man. He knows about us. Initially he had some trouble understanding this. But she had very tenderly assured him, and he has become comfortable about it now. He knows the intensity of our connection. And that it goes beyond his relationship with her. But that doesn't seem to bother him anymore. These are just some of my stories.

A. G.: *Revathi, how have your relationships panned out?*

R: Most of my relationships outside of my marriage, whether of love or sex or both, have been rather fleeting. They are neither concrete nor well defined. Perhaps I like it like that, since, till date, I have felt that my primary relationship with Subir is the most important one. Whenever things seem to go a little awry, I step back into that zone. This relationship has always been my comfort—like family. Yes, family can be difficult, but it is, after all, family. It feels uncomfortable to have a mad kind of love for someone else. I think I will just call it desire. I am not sure. There have been cases where I didn't even like the guy that much and I cringed at my girlishness, but the body and the heart just defied logic and I felt super attracted to him.

While I have had sexual connections with many of Subir's lovers, he has only rarely had that with my lovers. It is a veritable tightrope-walk at times, but it has also led to a sense of a deeply felt freedom. While in some encounters, our feelings are similar, in some others, they are not. Sometimes, I think, people like us miss the emotional part when it is too sexual, and miss the pure ecstasy of sex when we get emotional. A balance is desirable.

The only relationships that have withstood the vagaries of time are the ones where friendships already existed. There are one or two where the sex, which is not exclusive, brought in a friendship that is rather exclusive and has matured over time.

A. G.: Subir, what kind of conversations do you have with Revathi about these relationships? Are there rules?

S: Revathi is a very permissive person. She has always responded to my needs, my fantasies, and my attraction towards other people. She also understands my propensity towards quickly developing a soft corner for people with whom I connect. While I mostly fall for women, I have had crushes on men too. Sexually, Revathi and I have opened up to almost all of them, and continue to have strong sexual relations with most of them. While that often includes threesomes, we also engage individually.

My conversations about these relationships with Revathi are sometimes strongly sexual and kinky. They could happen after a threesome, or even after our individual experiences. Or just suddenly out of nowhere. I derive a lot of sexual pleasure from talking to her about her individual experiences. It can be very stimulating for me. The thing that really triggers me sexually is to intimately feel her sexual pleasure. I think nothing pleasures me more than the experience of that. I like to watch her being pleasured, by another man or woman. I also like her watching me having pleasure and having pleasure together. The intensity of that pleasure is liberating; the intoxication of that freedom is addictive.

I don't know if we have any set rules about these conversations—we do it spontaneously. Maybe having a few rules is not a bad idea.

R: But Subir, there is one rule, isn't there? Share as much as you can, confide, don't hide, avoid secrecy. I think that's the rule. You, of course, are more inclined to sharing and going into details. I can do without sharing too.

Aru, I also feel guilty sometimes, even though Subir acts quite cool, when I discern some emotional insecurity. I can never be sure whether they come from me or him but they are there. I often think that the problem arises due to exclusion. So, we have consciously tried to include each other in our individual sojourns as well. Also, over the years, I have begun to be cool about any relationship that he has as long as he nurtures our relationship as well.

But I also want to say this: for Subir, the journey is always an act of friendship where the boundary of friendship extends to include sexual relations. There would be a process of knowing the other person. Many who met me earlier have thought of me to be his friend—not a partner and definitely not wife. It is a different kind of world that he seems to be creating where there is space for fun, madness, and his kind of love. Sometimes they have bordered on obsession and I have been witness to that. At the outset, I had misgivings and much insecurity with his other lovers, but ultimately, I seem to have become more friendly with them than even he is. That has been my way of experiencing this.

A. G.: *What do these kinds of sexual encounters bring to your lives?*

S: For me, well, I have found my 'thing'. That's what they call it, don't they? 'What's your thing?' they ask. I think this is my 'thing'. If I had not experienced this with Revathi, perhaps I would have kept looking for it all my life and never known it. I don't know if that is true for Revathi though—well, she will have to answer that. Maybe not exactly in the way it is for me; maybe in some other way, it is as important for her. These sexual experiences and getting to know my own sexuality through them, have got me to a sexually happy place. I can't say I don't crave for more. I do. On some days, I feel this craving may be the flipside. On one hand, I could have been completely sexually frustrated if I wasn't here, and on the other, being here, I want more. It is addictive, and I have quite an appetite for it. To be honest, it can sometimes be a bit of a double-edged sword, but not having known it would have made me a different person.

A. G.: *And for you, Revathi?*

R: For me, they bring a lot—thoughtfulness, mindfulness, mutual trust, honesty, giving space to each other, making space for other individuals or even other couples, respect towards people irrespective of gender or sexuality, respect for the consent of everyone involved, creating a calm and easy atmosphere. All of this—it is really a whole different kind of living.

A. G.: *What about jealousy and insecurity? Revathi?*

R: Yes, most definitely, I have felt it, many times over. It is really hard to deal with. Jealousy can be sexual or otherwise, expressed in all forms possible. Insecurity is the worst feeling which causes one to feel jealous. I don't think I had handled it well in the beginning. I would cry a lot, shout, and throw things. As time passes, one just learns to deal with it. Probably, Subir has done enough to make me feel emotionally reassured.

S: For me, the journey with jealousy and insecurity is a real complex and extremely interesting one. I think this journey has truly helped me understand myself a bit better.

Somewhere, at the centre of my emotion of jealousy was a very strong image—the sexual image of my partner with another person. It was an obsessive image. The more I tried to look away from it, the more painful it would become. The more detailed it would become. I kept spiralling into darkness, trying to fight this image. The force of the image was so strong that I was coerced to surrender. One day, I took a deep breath and instead of looking away, I looked at the image. And something happened. I slowly realized that it was not the sexual nature of the image that made me anxious or want to fight it and look away. My struggle was with myself, with my sense of identity. I had never identified myself as someone who may actually find these images fascinating, exciting, deeply erotic! Doesn't that make me a 'pervert', I wondered. I was scared, perhaps repulsed, by the idea of looking at myself as one. But as I gave in to those images, I started discovering a whole new world for the first time. I never imagined that I would end up finding the images of my partner being sexually pleasured by other people so pleasurable.

Once that switch happened in my head, my relationship with the emotion of jealousy and insecurity changed. I wouldn't say that since then, it's always been a joyous ride. Jealousy is an unpredictable monster. It can raise its head anytime. It's natural and it's lurking just around the corner. But today, perhaps I am in a better place with it. Revathi always assures me of a strong sense of compatibility, which helps me with my insecurity. I think she finds my connection with her pleasure, quite pleasurable too.

A. G.: Is being honest difficult? Revathi, what would you say?

R: Honesty is difficult when you fear hurting your loved one. Even if you are in an open relationship, I feel it is hard to be completely honest. But it is the best policy, provided we have mutual understanding and believe in the principle of openness.

However, honesty is different from being transparent and pouring out all the details. When I sleep with someone else and I talk about it with Subir, I feel guilty. I am afraid and I assume that he will be jealous. That makes it even more complicated. It is one thing to know that your partner has just slept with someone else but it's different when one goes into the details of the sexual encounter. My partner might be able to visualize and feel the energy, yet miss his own presence there. Jealousy may creep in. It is easier to be honest if you are confident that your partner is able to handle it.

S: To be honest, so far, I have not found being honest difficult. In fact, I find the idea of not being honest more difficult. It's a lot of hard work. There's a lot of joy in being able to share almost anything with your partner. But perhaps, that's also not such a great idea always. The other person may not be ready for that honesty. Many people have told me this. Once, I had been to a therapist. I was going through very difficult times. She told me that I had a tendency of oversharing. That may not always be helpful. This is something that I have been trying to understand. But not being completely honest still doesn't look like an option to me. Of course, Revathi would be a better judge of how honest I really am.

A. G.: *What are some of the challenges, Subir?*

S: Sometimes, Revathi and I relive our sexual experiences with other people when we are having sex with each other. On some days, we are in heavenly sync. But on others, we are not. Then we talk about the reasons as to why we are not. Perhaps it is something that is bothering both of us. Sometimes, Revathi wants to hold on to an experience close to her heart. She may not be ready to share. I can be impatient. I want to get into the zone too quickly. And that causes a gap. I feel sad when that happens. When we fail to click sometimes. As pleasurable as it may sound—and most of the times it is—there are moments when we can also feel quite volatile, very vulnerable. There are a few silent days. Days of pent-up grief and pain. During those times, our conversations are about the very fundamental aspects of our relationship. What we mean to each other. What this whole thing means to us. To perhaps critically see why we were not in sync. We ask whether our encounters still mean the same thing for us individually. We try to connect again.

A. G.: *What about the problems you face, Revathi?*

R: To be brutally honest, if I were in a traditional relationship, I would have probably divorced my husband long ago. Being in this different kind of relationship, that has both modern and traditional expressions to it, is a huge boon. But I still struggle with basic questions and doubts. I often find relationships and myself in relationships emotionally exacting. Even debilitating. In some ways, I am still the traditional person like my mother, who doesn't give up. Yet I don't give in either. Subir and I have both struggled a lot to even arrive at these encounters, keep our sanity around them, and also keep the sanctity of our relationship in the storm that might ensue sometimes. We attempt to keep the excitement within our relationship and still do what we want in the outside world.

I don't know how successful or unsuccessful we are in this, but it's a work in progress. The inherent dominating nature of men and the tilted power equation—I feel those more outside of sex. Cohabitation can be beautiful but is still laden with complications. So, I question—even if one manages to think differently and act differently, can one really sustain the space for their primary partner all the way?

A. G.: Do you think you are polyamorous, Revathi?

R: I don't know if I am polyamorous. I surely believe in polyamory but I may be quite short of that right now. There is a boundary that I have to cross for that. Though I operate as an individual, I think like a couple. Polyamory, I think, is a journey of the individual. But polyamory is also about loving people around you—which I do. So am I polyamorous?

A. G.: And what would you say, Subir—are you polyamorous?

S: Maybe I am. Earlier, I used to think that to be polyamorous I had to love everyone equally. But Revathi is the centre of my life. After talking to you, when I understood that in polyamorous relationships, too, we can have central, primary partners, then I figured—yes, I am a polyamorous person by nature. I may not be practising it a whole lot, or all the time. But yes, I am. You tell me, am I not?

SECTION III

LIGHTHOUSES IN THE MIST

The great revelation perhaps never did come.
Instead there were little daily miracles, illuminations,
matches struck unexpectedly in the dark.

—Virginia Woolf

13

THE STATE'S CARROT, THE STATE'S STICK: THE LEGAL FRAMEWORK

As a polyamorous person, I have never thought of how the laws of the land may affect my life. But when one is a minority among dominant practices, it is important to know and understand the scope of the state's guarantee of equal rights as citizens and protection against discrimination. It is also wise to be cautious of the state's participation in the enforcement of the conventional. In recent discussions with other polyamorous people, I realized almost everyone is exactly in the same place as me—blissfully ignorant. Our extent of comprehension of the law and participating in any kind of advocacy was restricted to the struggle to decriminalize homosexuality in the country with Article 377. Even there, what we mostly did was write slogans, draw posters, and march, guided ably by our friends from the legal profession and activists who led the movement. So, I decided to speak with two lawyers, Dolashree Mysoor and Arvind Narrain, both based in Bengaluru, to find out exactly where the law was, with respect to the lives of polyamorous people.

DOLASHREE MYSOOR

My first conversation was with Dolashree Mysoor. Dolashree teaches law. Her research interests include constitutional studies, law and politics in India, disability studies, queer theory, political philosophy, and feminist legal theory. Her work also focuses on law and marginalization. She is currently working on a project that deals with promoting access to public spaces such as parks.

(A. G.: Arundhati Ghosh / D. M.: Dolashree Mysoor)

A. G.: I want to begin by asking you—legally, what should polyamorous people be aware of? What are the specific laws or gaps in our legal system that can impact polyamorous people?

D. M.: That's actually quite a big question. We don't have any laws that protect polyamorous people. But there are two sides to this. Because there are no laws, you don't have rights, you don't have protections, you don't have claims. On the other side, not having laws is also useful. It limits the state's role in and control of your life. You live in the shadow of the law, where you still have a lot more individual control over what you can do. The state can't interfere and that's valuable too.

Not having rights, protection, or claims can impact us in many ways. Imagine there is a polyamorous person living with two different partners, sharing the week between them. To fall within protection of the law against domestic violence, they would have to prove that they are in a 'relationship in the nature of marriage' with one person. So, their ability to claim protections against domestic violence will not arise in this case because neither of the two relationships will be considered a domestic relationship within the law. The law is understood within the monogamous framework. Also, if there is a partner's partner—a metamour—who is violent towards them, there is no protection from that in the law against domestic violence. However, I often tell polyamorous people who face violence, that they can also use laws against assault and battery under general criminal law which do not require proving the existence of a domestic relationship.

Another challenge with the law, for polyamorous people, is the area of child-rearing. Let's say I'm polyamorous and married to one partner, but I have a child with another partner to whom I'm not married. In this case, if you are tracking the lineage through the birth-mother and birth-father, it is fine, but if the law does it on the basis of whom I'm married to, then we do have a problem. Again, what happens to the various questions of making decisions for the child's life, where they will live, how they will share time? It gets complicated. When monogamous married people with children get divorced, their parental rights are quite clear. But it is much more complex in the case of polyamory and there is no guidance from the law. Unless the three partners are living together or creating their own set of mutually agreeable rules, this will be difficult to work out legally. And if there is some kind of falling out among them, there are no laws where parental rights are protected.

But let's see the other side of legalities entering our lives—with the laws around adultery. Adultery is a ground for separation and divorce. Until very recently, it used to be a criminal offense, and was decriminalized only in 2018. The way the law is framed here is that it is about one man 'stealing' another man's wife, who is deemed the property of the man. So, even if you are consenting adults, you could be subject to prosecution for this. Especially if you're a married woman and you have a male partner outside of marriage. That male partner too becomes liable. Luckily, the criminality part has been done away with—a little too late, in my opinion. But the issue of adultery as a ground for divorce remains and that is the problem of living within the law. When you have a law, it tends to regulate each and every individual action because you have given in to state control.

But it is not just 'adding' polyamory to current laws that can change things. The key problem with all our various marriage laws and family laws is that the framework within which they are conceptualized is, firstly, monogamous, and secondly, assumes that the family is natal and nuclear. Except the Islamic law on marriage that allows polygamy for men, all the others—the Hindu Marriage Act, the Christian Marriage Act, the Parsi Marriage Act—are steeped in heteronormative monogamy. Every definition within these laws assumes that two people—one man and one woman—are married and live together, and this monogamous arrangement informs all the laws around the unit including property and inheritance laws, laws guiding child-rearing, and divorce and maintenance.

The moment the unit consists of more than one partner, the problems with definitions and conferring responsibilities begin.

Let's take maintenance-related obligations for, say, psychosocial disability. In the case of polyamory, how will the law decide who does it? Who has the obligations of care? In a situation of a medical emergency, who gets to be the medical proxy and take those decisions at the hospital? Will it then require all polyamorous people to always declare a primary partner and have that registered with the government? This has been sorted out by the National Mental Healthcare Act where individuals with psychosocial disabilities and mental illness can appoint a representative. But where a person doesn't do this, the situation gets complex. Typically, hospitals will reinforce monogamous structures or natal family structures in such cases. This holds true for end-of-life decisions as well.

There are other problems I see when it comes to opening up the law to include the idea of polyamory. The definition of polyamory is different for various polyamorous people. We don't agree on a single definition. There can be very different kinds of relationships—a 'V' with three people, or a quad with four, or just a solo polyamorous person. Concepts such as marriage within polyamory and the idea of the chosen family are complex. So, what counts as marriage and what does not, will need to be defined sharply for the purpose of the law, as will separation and divorce. That would again differ depending on how many people are involved and at what level. If there are children involved, then the definition of parenthood will have to be fixed.

The fluid nature of polyamorous relationships poses a unique challenge to the law. How will the state create uniform standards and legal formulations for all this diversity and relationships in motion? What kind of marriage is worthy of being considered legal? All of these questions come up when one engages with the law. These are questions where the law will struggle. Deciding on the correct scope and extent of regulation would raise many debates. So, it's not as simple as just improving the law. There is a need for an overhaul of mono-normativity if we must engage legally with polyamory. Even the more recent proposals that have come for reforms, and in family law, are still very much grounded in monogamy.

In many ways, I think that polyamory itself is a test case or a limit case for laws on marriage and family. It pushes this idea of the monogamous understanding of marriage and family to a point where it doesn't hold any more. You will have to revamp the very fundamentals of marriage itself and focus more on individual autonomy. You're no longer talking about a state that is giving you a set idea of marriage that is between two people—you are now saying that it is left to a number of individuals to direct their marriages in the way that they want. That is something that the state still hasn't been able to grasp. Also, there are notions of fidelity and longevity intrinsically tied to marriage which may pose a challenge to the inclusion of polyamory. Polyamory disrupts these ideas. The law will have to deal with these disruptions. In some sense, the entire enterprise of family law will have to be equipped to handle two things in a more wholesome manner—(1) marriage itself; and (2) non-marital partnerships.

I want to mention one particularly interesting aspect. When the natal family cannot provide the kind of support we need, that's when chosen families come up. When you look at laws in the queer spaces in India, you notice an acceptance of the Gharana system among the Hijra communities, which symbolizes chosen family in some respects. So, there is already a model of the chosen family as being distinct from the natal nuclear family. It may not be in the mainstream, but we can understand how to conceptualize, establish, and sustain these kinds of chosen families from this example. In a polyamorous family, you may have people in different kinds and degrees of relationships with each other. Some may be sexual and some may be purely emotional. The point is to figure out how to accommodate this while defining the chosen family and still make domestic rights, child rights, and financial rights available to the members.

The linking up of sex, romance, and marriage is a major problem for polyamory. In fact, under today's legal scheme, we don't have an articulation or imagination of an 'asexual' or 'aromantic' marriage. The law, too, assumes that sex and romance are intrinsic to the idea of a marriage. We've been unable to even criminalize marital rape—a violent marriage that the law should not permit. Polyamory challenges this basic assumption of monogamy—that sex is integral to a relationship with a partner, and is restricted to that partner alone. Decriminalizing adultery is a good step, but we need to move beyond this if we want to be inclusive of both queer and poly interests. In some ways, this is an issue where queer and polyamorous interests intersect to challenge mono-normativity in the law.

There are some who do take the position that non-monogamy has created more harm to certain vulnerable groups. Now, that is true. It is empirically true that Muslim women have been at a disadvantageous position because of the way polygamy has been included in Islamic law. There is a possibility of desertion or neglect of a partner when you include something like polygamy or polyamory within the law. But that alone is not sufficient to say that we ought not look beyond monogamy as a viable option. The fact that this harm happens is something that has to be regulated by law, as opposed to not including a non-monogamous framework.

So that's where I would start off—with a discussion on the law itself.

A. G.: As a lawyer, what are some of the areas that you feel are important for conversations to begin, within the legal system, in order to create a more protected space for polyamorous people?

D. M.: I would focus on three key areas. The first is a conversation on protection from domestic violence. We have already discussed that.

The second aspect is that of children. There is a sense that if children are involved in a polyamorous situation, there will be child sexual abuse. This is a dangerous assumption. That's simply not true. It's like the prevailing prejudice against gay parents. You may have bad apples in any situation. But they cannot be seen as the whole community. Mono hetero families have not been able to curtail child sexual abuse in any case.

So, with children, I think the most important aspect is how they will be raised. Today, this is determined in a patriarchal way in monogamous families, which typically tend to assume that the child will follow the religion of the father, take the name of the father. When you think of children from polyamorous families, some of these entrenched notions will have to be broken around child-rearing. I don't think polyamorous communities are so fixated on the idea of longevity. But parenthood is thought through from the point of the stability that longevity brings. So, when a child in a polyamorous situation is living with more than one parent, how responsibilities are understood will require some thought. There is a whole world to unpack there.

Thirdly, finances. Money and property are important, particularly in vulnerable contexts. When it comes to inheritance, the easy way to do this, in the absence of such laws guiding the lives of polyamorous people, is to create a will. I tell this to every polyamorous person. Make a will. But in the case of polyamory, how property should be divided if people fall out of marriages, or inherit it if one person dies without a will, has to be brought within the law. Again, this challenges the monogamous understanding of property devolution in the case of inheritance. For example, consider a situation where I'm not a birth-parent but played the role of a parent to a child. They are not legally adopted by me either. If I die without a will, my property will not go to this child even if that's what I wanted. This can happen outside of polyamorous situations also, but with polyamory, it becomes more complex. Insistence on wills is probably a good way to proceed on this matter from a legal perspective.

Another aspect of finance is in relation to insurance where, today, mostly only parents, spouses, and children can be beneficiaries. Forget adding polyamorous partners to the mix, I cannot nominate a friend or any other member of my family. That's the industry standard. I cannot understand why it is so because ultimately it is my money and I should be able to nominate whoever I want.

Finally, we need to legally include the concept of a chosen family. Many people think of marriage laws as the main thing affecting polyamorous people. But, in my view, the marriage problem is not the only question we should be focusing on. Instead, legal reforms should work towards understanding the alternatives to natal families, like chosen families.

A. G.: Since we understand the dangers of the state entering our private and personal lives, I was wondering whether there are ways in which self-regulation can work as checks and balances in the polyamorous world?

D. M.: This brings me to the question of who the polyamorous community in India is, and how we define it. Mostly, we have been talking of the urban upper-middle-class English-speaking people living across a few cities and towns, perhaps. That is a very small number, and even among them the definitions of polyamory are very different. A few cities have groups where people identify themselves as polyamorous. But that's about it. There is no large collective movement and advocacy around it. 'Polyamorous community' in itself is a bit of a misnomer. We know nothing of what is happening outside of our known spaces. What is the language of people in rural regions who feel they are polyamorous? How do they express or identify themselves in terms of their relationships? We have not even begun to ask these questions. So, the question of a larger collective universe of polyamorous people is still far off. And until that is reckoned with, self-regulation of a larger community is a moot point. This is because self-regulation also requires some notion of a community. Today, we don't know what this 'community' is outside urban metropolitan areas.

However, where there are collectives, self-regulation within them is important. It is important to have some basic rules that protect the safety and privacy of everyone in that group and provide access to these spaces for vulnerable folks. Make sure there's no sexual harassment. Make sure nobody outs anyone. What we can also do as a collective is talk to each other, be open about our struggles, and share grievances. We could look for solutions together this way too. Grievances could be settled through a process of listening. But this is largely dependent on the individuals involved. In some senses, self-regulation is a concept that relies on the hope that people will engage in it and be good. There are no guarantees that this will work effectively. So, we do need some guardrails even within communities. But, this does not mean we need to involve the law here. Maybe some things require legal protection, like sexual harassment, caste-based discrimination, and violence. Laws exist on this front already—we just need to make use of them. But the broad contours of regulating the polyamorous community's activity itself need not be subject to legal regulation.

ARVIND NARRAIN

Arvind is a legal expert who has been involved in research, writing, and practice related to law and social concerns. His interests are in constitutionalism, human rights, legal history, and queer rights. He is currently in the process of doing his PhD on 'Mapping the Elements of an Ambedkarite Jurisprudence' at the National Law School of India University (NLSIU). He is the author and co-editor of *Law Like Love: Queer Perspectives on Law* as well as the co-author of *Breathing Life into the Constitution*. He is also the author of *India's Undeclared Emergency: Constitutionalism and the Politics of Resistance*. He was a part of the team of lawyers challenging Section 377 of the Indian Penal Code right from the high court in 2009, to the Supreme Court in 2018.

(A. G.: Arundhati Ghosh / A. R.: Arvind Narrain)

A. G.: What are the key things that a polyamorous person should be aware of in terms of their position in the legal system in this country?

A. N.: I would like to begin at a different point, which is, why would I be interested in the polyamory question itself? Being a part of the queer community, right from the very beginning, I realized that discussions from within the community always challenged the notion of both heteronormativity as well as the presumption that people are going to be couples living together forever. That was my starting point. People were already living these lives. Challenging the law on this—the struggle with Section 377 of the Indian Penal Code served the function of bringing the importance of the queer discourse into the open, and also became a way to talk about police harassment and violence.

But then the deeper question on this is what the goal of this movement against Section 377 was and who was going to benefit. What are the forms of relationships which would be liberated with this struggle? By challenging the law, we challenged heteronormativity in all its dimensions—that a couple meant a man and a woman, the idea that two persons in love had to be together for the rest of their lives, that some relationships are not acceptable, or not recognized within the framework of the law. Many years ago, I had read an article by journalist Kaveri Bamzai who had succinctly stated that Section 377 was a symbol of all that is wrong with our sexual universe. Our struggle had to represent the diversity of the queer community, including polyamorous people in their range of relationalities. People had to see Section 377 as an attack both on their sexual and romantic expression, as well as multiple expressions of love. This had to be our first battle.

Here I want to mention that in the *Naz Foundation v Government of NCT of Delhi* judgment in 2009, Chief Justice Ajit Prakash Shah and Justice S. Muralidhar had cited what Pandit Nehru said while moving the 'Objectives Resolution' in 1946: 'Words are magic things often enough, but even the magic of words sometimes cannot convey the magic of the human spirit and of a Nation's passion....' The judges concluded that the foundation of the Indian Constitution lay in its inclusiveness. Inclusiveness, non-discrimination, equality, and dignity were the four key pillars of this judgment. 'It cannot be forgotten that discrimination is [the] antithesis of equality and that it is the recognition of equality which will foster the dignity of every individual,' they added.

Though the 2009 judgment was overturned in 2013, finally in 2018, the judgment came in favour of the community, decriminalizing homosexuality. However, the queer community did not wait for this judgment from the courts to live their lives—they continued to create what Stanley Cavell called 'little communities of love' throughout this time and the courts finally followed the community in decriminalizing queer lives. This battle was not just about being able to practise what the law called 'carnal intercourse against the order of nature' in the privacy of one's home. It was about dignity of all human expressions and the freedom to articulate them. It was recognition of diversity too.

I think the battle against Section 377 was the first phase. It was a battle for the recognition of diverse ways of living. The second phase is about the right to relationship recognition—the quest for marriage equality which is still work in progress. Perhaps the next phase would be for polyamorous people to demand what they seek—whether it is recognition, protection, dignity, or acceptance. This could be one way to think of developing the struggle in phases.

In a legal sense, that would be a more practical way to think because polyamory challenges the idea of both heteronormativity and marriage. So, logically, it should come right after the first two phases. For polyamorous people, there will be three things to pin their arguments on. The first is the concept of dignity in the right to make choices about one's individual personal life. Second is the notion of equality, and third is the right to expression. However, while the legal struggle goes from one phase to another, people will continue to live and practise as per their desires which form the groundwork—the lived experiences. The social and cultural articulations have to happen before the legal articulation.

(**Background on Section 377 of the Indian Penal Code:** The section was introduced in 1861 during the British rule of India. Modelled on the Buggery Act 1533, it makes sexual activities 'against the order of nature' illegal. On 6 September 2018, the Supreme Court of India ruled that the application of Section 377 to consensual homosexual sex between adults was unconstitutional, 'irrational, indefensible and manifestly arbitrary', but that Section 377 remains in force relating to sex with minors, non-consensual sexual acts, and bestiality.

Portions of the section were first struck down as unconstitutional with respect to gay sex by the Delhi High Court in July 2009. That judgment was overturned by the Supreme Court of India on 11 December 2013 in *Suresh Kumar Koushal v Naz Foundation*. The court held that amending or repealing Section 377 should be a matter left to Parliament, not the judiciary. On 6 February 2016, a three-member bench of the court reviewed curative petitions submitted by the Naz Foundation and others, and decided that they would be reviewed by a five-member constitutional bench. On 24 August 2017, the Supreme Court upheld the right to privacy as a fundamental right under the Constitution in the landmark Puttaswamy judgment. The court also called for equality and condemned discrimination, stated that the protection of sexual orientation lies at the core of the fundamental rights, and that the rights of the LGBT population are real and founded on constitutional doctrine. This judgment was believed to imply the unconstitutionality of Section 377.

In January 2018, the Supreme Court agreed to hear a petition to revisit the 2013 Naz Foundation judgment. On 6 September 2018, the court ruled unanimously in *Navtej Singh Johar v Union of India* that Section 377 was unconstitutional 'in so far as it criminalises consensual sexual conduct between adults of the same sex'. The judgment was given by a five-judge bench comprising the then-Chief Justice of India, Dipak Misra; Justices R. F. Nariman, D. Y. Chandrachud, A. M. Khanwilkar, and Indu Malhotra.)

A. G.: *When I was in college thirty years ago, we didn't even have the language for our queerness. But today, if there is a book on queer people, I know I will see so many brave folks out there speaking for themselves and their community in the book. The struggle has taken this long to get here. Polyamory is at the place, I feel, where queer politics was thirty years ago. It's still such a taboo; it is dangerous to be out for the fear of discrimination.*

A. N.: In Gayle Rubin's hierarchy of sexual value from the article 'Thinking Sex: Notes for a Radical Theory of the Politics of Sexuality', homosexual people with long-term relationships have a much higher place than, say, transsexual people and sex workers. I am not sure where she would put polyamorous people. But I suppose they would be towards the bottom of the pyramid. This is a kind of class system topped by married and child-producing heterosexual people.

A. G.: What are some impacts of the lack of laws for polyamorous people?

A. N.: The only things the law recognizes are relationships based on blood and marriage. That makes for many practical problems. Suppose, someone has an accident. No medical decision can be made by anyone who has a long-term relationship with that person. Only those in ties of blood and marriage can make such a decision. This affects people not just in polyamorous relationships, of course. The next of kin question is a problem for many people like this who do not have monogamous heterosexual relationships.

The same applies to adoption rules. Or say, inheritance laws. The entire legal system is based on two pillars as far as these relationships and sexualities are concerned—heteronormativity and monogamy. So, everything we are talking about today is based on those two factors. They have to change. There could be a question about whether we do that in stages or together within our struggles. And this puts everything under question, like, where do your civil and labour rights stand? Where does the workman's compensation go? Who gets to adopt and be parents? The struggles around this are also quite diverse. On one end, we have the Uniform Civil Code in Uttarakhand that needs people who are living in to register, or else they will get arrested and fined. On the other end, in Chennai, at the Madras High Court, there's a petition in which the court has asked the government to respond to the question as to whether a deed of 'familial association' between any two people—meaning irrespective of their gender or sexuality—can be registered. This is a contractual agreement between any two people and will the government recognize it—(this) is the question of the court.

A. G.: What are the key things that you feel the polyamorous community should work on to build advocacy in the legal area?

A. N.: In the polyamorous community, I think you should truly build on the struggle against Section 377, which embodied a range of perspectives of authentic sexual behaviours challenging the hetero–mono ways of being. Similarly, it is important to concentrate on the minority judgment of Chief Justice D. Y. Chandrachud and Justice Sanjay Kishan Kaul in the more recent marriage judgment for queer people. They held that constitutional authorities should carve out a regulatory framework to recognize the civil union of adults in a same-sex relationship. They held that the right to enter into a union cannot be restricted on the basis of sexual orientation. Discrimination on the basis of sexual orientation is violative of Article 15 of the Constitution, the chief justice said. They also made it clear that relationship rights flowed from Article 21, which states that no person shall be deprived of personal liberty; Article 19c, which states that there will be freedom of expression and right to form unions; and Article 25, that gives freedom of conscience. For the minority judgment, the fact that there is no statute is not of consequence, because the right to be recognized in a relationship is a dimension of these constitutional provisions. The minority opinion is clear that the 'bonds or relationships nourish the emotional and spiritual dimension of our humanity and are important in and of themselves'.

It's surely not the last that we have heard of the dissent of Justices Chandrachud and Kaul. Justice Khanna, in his famous dissent in *ADM Jabalpur* (1976), had invoked the words of Charles Evan Hughes, the former chief justice of the US Supreme Court: 'A dissent in a court of last resort is an appeal to the brooding spirit of the law, to the intelligence of a future day, when a later decision may possibly correct the error into which the dissenting judge believes the court to have been betrayed.' This, therefore, could be the strongest basis—a starting point—for building a case for polyamorous people if they want recognition of relationships and marriages. There is enough space in this minority judgment to expand on the notion of equality and discrimination to include the demands of polyamorous people legally.

It is also important to build this case with data from the field. When we spoke of sexual violence against transgender people many years ago, no one listened. But then we went into research and collated all the data that there was. We, at the People's Union for

Civil Liberties (PUCL), published a report entitled 'Human Rights Violations Against the Transgender Community'. That made a huge difference. Now, no one can challenge the validity of whether transgender folks face sexual violence because there is documentary evidence. Similarly, polyamorous people should collect data on their lived realities, their experiences, their struggles, and collate it to build a case. This amount of work has to be put in first. One can't just do this as an additional aspect of the current marriage equality petitions. Once the work has been done and a case built, then we can go to the courts, stating that people are already living this way, building relationships this way—that is the reality in the society and it should be recognized. That would make for a strong case.

(Background on the marriage judgment of the Supreme Court of India on October 17, 2023: On 14 November 2022, two same-sex couples filed writ petitions in the Supreme Court, seeking legal recognition of same-sex marriages in India. The petitions were centred around the constitutionality of the Special Marriage Act, 1954 (the Act). The first petition was filed by Supriyo Chakraborty and Abhay Dang. The second petition was by Parth Phiroze Mehrotra and Uday Raj Anand.

The petitioners argue that Section 4(c) of the Act recognizes marriage only between a 'male' and a 'female'. This discriminates against same-sex couples by denying them matrimonial benefits such as adoption, surrogacy, employment, and retirement benefits. The petitioners asked the court to declare Section 4(c) of the Act unconstitutional. The plea has been tagged with a number of other petitions challenging other personal laws on similar grounds. The challenged enactments include the Hindu Marriage Act, 1955, and the Foreign Marriage Act, 1969. The petitioners argue that the non-recognition of same-sex marriage violates the rights to equality, freedom of expression, and dignity. They relied on *NALSA v Union of India* (2014) and *Navtej Singh Johar v Union of India* (2018) which recognized non-binary gender identities and guaranteed equal rights to homosexual persons.

Between November 2022 and January 2023, many similar

petitions from Delhi and Kerala High Courts were transferred to the Supreme Court. On 11 May 2023, the five-judge bench reserved judgment after ten days of hearings.

On 17 October 2023, the five-judge bench pronounced its verdict on petitions seeking marriage equality for LGBTQIA+ persons. The bench unanimously held that there was no fundamental right to marry and that the court could not recognize LGBTQIA+ persons' right to marry under the Special Marriage Act.)

A. G.: *How much should we allow the state to enter our lives? What should be our relationship with the state as far as laws and guiding our lives is concerned?*

A. N.: In a utopian situation, one could argue that we do not need the state in our lives, or that we do not need laws. Given that different people want different things—some want marriage and some don't, some want validity for relationships and some don't—one could even say we do need the state to play a role in this. But the world is unequal with unequal power dynamics between people. It is also true that people can be horrible to each other. So basic legal frameworks to regulate relationships and rights within those relationships are needed in society. Polyamorous people have to establish their lives at the ground level and then look at the laws that they need for regulation in the current moment. For example, if three people in a relationship share a house that belongs to one of them, and if that person dies, what happens to the house and the other two people—do they get thrown out? Domestic violence is another area of concern in polyamorous relationships. Like we have devised laws and proceedings for sexual harassment at the workspace, similar laws must be created for units of people living together in domestic situations. That will protect the vulnerable.

There's also the problem of over-regulation that does not allow for nuanced conversations, making everything black and white. We have to ensure that we continue to have conversations that may be both difficult and uncomfortable even with whatever regulation is there.

14

HOLDING SPACE: SUPPORT STRUCTURES
FOR POLYAMOROUS PEOPLE

Journeys with relationships are difficult. But sometimes, polyamorous folks find it tougher. The social support that is available to monoamorous people to share, vent, or seek solutions to issues that arise out of relationships, is not there for polyamorous people. It becomes hard to talk about feelings and difficulties since most people can be harsh and judgemental. 'Well, that's what you sowed—so now you reap!' is the subtext of many conversations. Therefore, like all groups that live tentatively on the margins of acceptability in society, polyamorous people must figure out their own support systems.

The first port of support that polyamorous people experience is often not their natal family and friends. Even when they may, in some cases, accept us as we are, they don't understand us. Other polyamorous people and support groups consisting of them, thus, become the most important part of the ecosystem that enables polyamorous folks to live safely, as fully as we can. These spaces bring people together to share experiences, challenges, and ways to cope. They provide hope when there are feelings of loneliness, rejection, being judged, or frustration. Just like the experiences of queer people, rejection from natal families, if we are out to them, has made polyamorous people hold on to these spaces tightly. People from support groups often become part of what we lovingly call our chosen family. They are there as shoulders to lean on, caregivers to call upon, and to provide safety nets for our emotional and psychological well-being.

The Bangalore Polycule is one such support group for polyamorous people in Bengaluru. Started in 2016, this group consists of about sixty to seventy members today, who are connected with each other through messaging apps. They also meet physically to discuss experiences, issues, look for answers, and just be with each other from time to time. While some members live openly polyamorous lives, many are not out due to fear of social ostracization and have disclosed their identity only within the group. There is a strong safety protocol in the group that enables a space that is protected for people who already feel vulnerable and marginalized. There are also strict rules for the process of being a member of the group. This includes filling in a form and responding to a series of questions by existing members in an interview. Only after being vetted can one become a member. Members have to sign on and abide by the safety protocols. Sometimes, groups like these can become grounds for predatory behaviour, so Bangalore Polycule takes its security measures very seriously. I have been part of the group for a while and through various conversations, learnt many aspects of the diverse journeys of polyamorous folks and the challenges they have overcome to pursue their chosen way of being.

The group organizes an annual day-long open-for-all polyamory festival in Bengaluru, called Anekapriyate, which means 'loving many' in Kannada. It is an attempt to raise awareness and build conversations around polyamory, and is now almost a decade old. Put together entirely by volunteers, the festival each year takes a slightly different form, depending on the time and skillsets of volunteers. There are performances, film screenings, quiz, board games, and discussion panels in this festival. It also includes 'Ask Me Anything' desks where volunteers answer any questions on polyamory and more engaged discussions take place. These discussions range from the many ways in which polyamory is practised within the larger umbrella of ethical non-monogamy, jealousy, break-ups, dating, safety, building chosen families, and stories of how various people navigate their lives of polyamory. It is a safe space to share insecurities, struggles, and vulnerabilities. The festival has, over the past years, seen a growing audience, especially young people who either practise polyamory, or are dating polyamorous people, or are just curious to understand different ways of being and starting to explore. There is also a merchandise desk with polyamory-themed stickers, mugs, zines, and badges. The courage, kindness, and camaraderie experienced in this festival is reassuring.

In a conversation about how the group started, one of the founders said, 'I had just started on my polyamorous journey, and I barely knew anyone who was polyamorous, whom I could reach out to for questions or for sharing experiences. Then I met someone who also identified as polyamorous. We decided to call one or two other polyamorous people we knew in the city, and we began to meet. After that, people started bringing friends and partners, and that evolved into a group that started meeting regularly.'

Speaking on how the group has changed since 2016, they said, 'At first, it was a very open-door policy; anyone could bring anyone in. However, over time, we realized that people often think a group of polyamorous people means an orgy. Sometimes, others just wanted to attend out of curiosity about polyamorous people; so, structures had to be put in place, and people volunteered for vetting and handling safety. Another change is that people have gotten to know each other more closely. For instance, there are some people, whom I met through the group, who are now my friends.'

I asked a few of the members why they felt a group like this was important and how it helped them. The first response came from someone who has been in the group since the beginning. She said, 'I think I'm one of those people who are still figuring out a lot about the polyamorous journey, and I always have questions about specific situations that I encounter. My monoamorous friends, however well-meaning, often do not know how to respond, and that is isolating. It's always a great experience for me to be able to throw out a question and get very nuanced and thoughtful answers from people in the group. Not from some *Ethical Slut* guidebook, but from something they, too, have experienced. Plus, it's a very normalizing experience, since there's a lot of judgement and messaging around monogamy being the ideal. It's only when

I'm hanging out with fellow polyamorous people that I realize how amazing it feels to be in a space where you don't have to constantly explain, justify, or hide your choices! Sometimes, it's not even the big conversations; it's all about the moments of companionship and casual conversation.'

Another member, who has joined more recently, said, 'Polyamorous people encounter unique challenges and situations that are often not addressed in traditional relationship advice. Bangalore Polycule is a source of community and belonging. Members can discuss their experiences, seek advice, and share insights with others who understand and live similar relational dynamics.'

Another member, who lives within a more traditional family system, said, 'It can be very isolating and lonely for a poly person to live, thrive, and work in a mono society and family. A support group is critical to maintain one's sanity and to be reassured that one is not in the wrong as far as poly orientation goes. It helps me as I see people who have similar thoughts. Being different from the mainstream can be a socially marginalizing experience and being with folks who are like-minded makes me stronger and happier.'

In response to my enquiry about what more a support group like this could do for our community, one person felt that there was a need to engage at a larger systemic level to fight against stigmatization. The community needs to find ways to engage with mental health professionals, media, and the law. Additionally, at a more micro level, when events are organized, they need to be more accessible in terms of language and location. Another member agreed that there was an urgent need to build awareness and remove the taboo around polyamory. Yet another member felt that beyond personal support, a group like Bangalore Polycule could benefit the community by bringing more conversations around alternative relationships to the public, combating myths and stigma, and advocating for legal recognition of polyamorous relationships. Through this, it could pave the way for legal protections and rights, creating a more inclusive world for polyamorous families.

It has been challenging for Bangalore Polycule to survive as a community. The members have been attacked many times, trolled online, and those who are public have been, at various points, ridiculed and humiliated. Yet they have courageously continued to support each other to ensure that there is a safe space for polyamorous people in the city. There is a need for more groups like these to come together. I hope they exist in other cities, in multiple language contexts, where people from all kinds of socio-economic backgrounds are welcome. There is always the danger of these groups becoming echo chambers of people from elite, English-speaking backgrounds. I have seen how aware Bangalore Polycule is of that danger, and they attempt at every possible situation to engage as many accessibility options as they can.

Just support groups are not enough. We need to have conversations with those we trust among our friends and family, even if they don't understand polyamory. Every time I visit a new country with unfamiliar cultures, eating habits, and social traditions, it is so much easier to navigate the unknowns if I have a local patiently explaining them and showing me around. Their guidance and kindness go a long way in my understanding of new terrains. As polyamorous people, we have this responsibility towards those who are close to us. Of course, this only makes sense if they are not hateful or have deeply embedded prejudices against us. If they are eager and open, it is possible to begin gentle conversations around how and why we are the way we are. In my life, I have seen that, over time, those who love us tend to make the effort to understand and accept us, no matter how freakish we may seem to the rest of the world. But it takes time and patience.

Continuing my search for existing support structures for polyamorous people, I wanted to speak to mental health professionals who provide much-needed care for those who are going through difficult times. But, there are very few therapists and almost no psychiatrists with experience of working with polyamorous people. It was a difficult task to find a few therapists whom I finally got to speak with, who were both queer and poly-affirmative.

Most of them felt that the mental health issues that polyamorous people bring to them are similar to those brought by monoamorous people and include struggles with anxiety, depression, insecurities, and disturbance caused by problems in relationships. In addition, neurodivergent polyamorous people face difficulties in understanding the complexities of their own neurodivergence as well as that of the people they are in relationships with. Tamanna, an ex-counsellor, mentioned that many of the polyamorous people who sought her help were queer, so their mental health issues had more to do with their gender and sexual identities.

Almost all of them mentioned that unravelling the threads of relationship issues becomes more complicated for polyamorous people because more than two people are involved. Tamanna shared how, since there is no playbook for polyamory, and very many permutations and combinations of relationship patterns and power dynamics exist, it becomes challenging for a therapist. She added that being polyamorous themselves may also not help therapists much because that, on its own, would not necessarily give them enough resources to help others. However, a few other therapists felt that having lived polyamorous lives, they were better-equipped to understand the issues when polyamorous people came for help. Another counsellor mentioned how, while for monoamorous relationship issues, it is possible to draw from earlier experiences, in the case of polyamorous relationships, a counsellor often has to start from scratch with every client, given the diversity of relationships.

Arulan P. S. Elai, a queer, polyamorous, kink-affirmative counselling psychologist and activist, shared that people who are exploring polyamory for the first time find it a confusing mix of emotions if they are dealing with a break-up while also entering new relationships. They felt that it was important to have someone guide and support them through shifts from mono to non-mono ways of being.

Speaking about how therapy can be a supportive safe space for polyamorous people, Arulan said that often, their therapy room is where people talk about their insecurities without feeling ashamed. This enables an attempt to understand the past emotional and relational wounds and messaging that may hamper their ability to trust new people who enter their lives. It is also a space to work towards being more aware of their own needs and communicating them to be fulfilled in healthier ways, thus enabling them to gauge their capacity to offer love and care in their multiple relationships.

When asked if mental health professionals today are ready to engage with polyamorous people, Arulan was doubtful whether most of them can be unbiased and non-discriminatory in providing professional support to non-monoamorous people. They mentioned that this distrust is born out of their own experiences of harmful comments from such professionals as well as what they have heard from clients. Arulan mentioned that their own therapist is non-monogamous and that has made them feel safe. Not once has she asked them to quit or be ashamed of being non-monoamorous. They added that they have another therapist who, while being monogamous herself, has been able to do the work of reading and understanding polyamory, hence Arulan feels comfortable talking to her too. These conversations, however, don't go into the depths of relationships, but that is fine with Arulan because they do have another therapist with whom they can do the deep work around being with multiple lovers.

Tamanna shared that no courses in India today provide study materials or resources for therapists to work with polyamorous people and that there is a huge gap in training. She also felt that while a therapist could learn through reading about polyamory and preparing themselves, this is a lot of work and investment of time. Given that the pool of polyamorous clients may not be that large, not many therapists would be inclined to put in the investment.

The conversations with the therapists lay bare all the difficulties polyamorous people have when it comes to getting psychological help. The lack of research and study adds to this gap. There is a need for the community to gather evidence, collect data, and build a case almost like 'proof of life' so that we can be seen as a legitimate community, as shared by lawyer Arvind Narrain in his interview with me for the chapter on legal matters in this book. We are at the right moment in time for such an exercise, with groups and collectives slowly coming together. So we should seriously consider consolidating our experiences.

15

WORDS WE MAKE: THE LANGUAGE OF POLYAMORY

When there are restrictions on love and relationships to stay within the tight boundaries of heteronormative and monoamorous frameworks, the mainstream language of love and relationship reflects those narrow contours. But as people explored different ways of loving, new words were added to languages. Over decades, the queer world has challenged understandings of gender and sexuality, thus adding many words to express their worlds.

In fact, the Hijra community (consisting of transgender folks in South Asia) have their own secret languages that they do not share with others. The Muslim Hijras use Hijra Farsi, with more than 10,000 words in their vocabulary. The Hindu Hijras, especially from the districts of Nadia, Medinipur, and Murshidabad in West Bengal in India and some parts of Bangladesh, use Ulti Bhasha or Gupti. These languages have words for sexual organs and erotic practices that are specific to the community, thereby expanding the world of pleasure and possibilities. Similarly, polyamory, remaining invisible and underground, has developed its own language quietly, covertly. As it happens in all communities that seek safety from discrimination, these additions to languages are often coded, with words and phrases having multiple meanings. They sometimes camouflage their true intent in front of the outer world. This also creates a playfulness of hide-and-seek within the language.

Unfortunately, most of my conversations with polyamorous people have been in English, and some in Bangla and Hindi. All the books I have read on polyamory are in English and from the Western world. I have not found too many spaces that invest time, effort, and resources into making place for the bouquet of Indian languages articulating sex and pleasure (the Agents of Ishq website is a notable exception). So, most of the words I have gathered, that are used in the polyamorous context, are in English. While this chapter stands limited by my own lack of skill beyond Bangla, English, and Hindi, it also bears witness to how little work has happened so far on research and writing about our lives in Indian languages.

But there is great hope. I do know of community members from the queer world who speak and live the worlds of other languages and are actively engaged in building a vocabulary that can accommodate their lived realities in their languages. Among the many that I have learnt from them, I particularly like the word 'roopantori', that is used for 'transgender' in Bangla. The word 'roop' in Bangla could mean beauty, image, visual presence, or form, depending on its usage. The word 'antar' in Bangla could mean shift, change, interval, or end, again depending on its usage. So 'roopantor' means 'transformation' and is used by the transgender community for themselves. This is one of the most poetic words that I have come across for the community in any language.

I hope there are people in the polyamorous community, too, who are actively creating words and expressions in various languages. I use 'bahumanorath' in Bangla for 'polyamory'. 'Bahu' is 'many' and 'manorath', loosely translated from Bangla, is 'heart's desire'. I heard the two words together for the first time in the song 'Bahu manorathe saju abhisare', meaning, 'I decorate myself with many desires (for a rendezvous with my lover)', penned by Rituparno Ghosh for their film *Memories in March* (2011). This song, as mentioned by Debasish Bhattacharya in his article entitled 'Bahu manorathe saju abhisare', (Learningandcreativity.com), is written in broken dialects of Sanskrit, Hindi, Maithili, Brajabuli, and Bangla. It strongly resembles verses from Rabindranath Tagore's collection of poems entitled *Bhanusingher Padabali*, that narrates the love story of Radha and Krishna. I joined the words together as 'bahumanorath' for polyamory in Bangla because it evoked the essence of Ghalib's 'Hazaron Khwahishein Aisi'. Thus, a polyamorous person, for me, is 'bahumanorathi'—a person who practises 'bahumanorath'. I also really like the Kannada word 'anekapriyate' discussed earlier.

Some words, like 'saut' in Hindi, meant for a co-wife in the context of a polygamous man's many wives, or the Bangla 'shoteen', carry deeply patriarchal and misogynistic connotations. Therefore, one has to be careful when looking for words from within our own vocabularies. The decisions to reuse some of those will need to be prefaced with a firm intent of reclaiming the articulation sans the burdens. I think there is a treasure trove in the vocabulary that is being created by queer and polyamorous people in various languages. A trained linguist could build a whole archive with that!

I will share some English words that have been coined by polyamorous communities across the world. I have already used many of them in the earlier chapters while discussing the practice of polyamory. But here, I want to have them listed all together for easy access. These come almost entirely from Western scholarship and are used frequently in the Indian context as well. The need to share this arises out of the desire to be able to speak with more ease from the polyamorous world to the monoamorous one.

Since a large part of the polyamorous world overlaps with the queer world, there are many words here which are common to both. Since these are definitions I have come to understand from reading and talking to various people over the past few years, their sources are many and scattered. Given that the language is evolving, words enter and leave the vocabulary routinely. While some words have many synonyms that different people use, sometimes, the same word is used in slightly varied ways in different contexts. Therefore, my suggestion would be to take this list as an introductory resource within polyamory, that does not claim to be either exhaustive or up to date.

Let us begin at the beginning. While I have already explained what I understand by monoamory, monogamy, polyamory, and polygamy at the very beginning of this book, just a quick refresher here because these words form the spine of the vocabulary.

Polyamory: The Greek 'poly' meaning 'many', and the Latin 'amor' meaning 'love', come together to describe the intent, ability, and practice of nurturing various relationships of love with or without sexual intimacies, with the consent of all involved.

Monoamory: The Greek 'mono' meaning 'single', and the Latin 'amor' meaning 'love', come together to describe the intent, ability, and practice of nurturing one relationship of love, almost always with sexual intimacies. When this happens more than once and a person moves from one partner to another, it is termed as 'sequential' or 'serial' monoamory.

The Greek word 'gamy' refers to marriage, so 'monogamy' just means being married to a single person at a time, and 'polygamy' means having multiple spouses. Within polygamy, 'polyandry' refers to the practice of a woman having many husbands and 'polygyny' to a man having many wives. Often, people use monogamy for monoamory, which can be confusing. It is important to note here that in many instances, polyamory is also referred to as ethical non-monogamy or consensual non-monogamy. However, this is not quite correct because ethical or consensual non-monogamy is an umbrella term for the various ways in which people can challenge monogamy. The words 'ethical' or 'consensual' are added to distinguish it from 'cheating' or any other form of deception. Polyamory is only one of the ways in which ethical or consensual non-monogamy can be practised. There are many other ways of practising ethical or consensual non-monogamy, like swinging, casual sex, and polygamy.

I have divided these words into five sets for easy understanding of their interconnected meanings. The first set of words refers to the various types of structures and formations within the large polyamorous world. The second set consists of words by which people identify their gender, sexuality, mode of romance, and sexual preferences. The third set consists of the various practices within polyamory. The fourth set describes the specific roles people play in the various formulations of polyamorous relationships. The fifth set refers to some of the other terms that describe feelings, rules, and policies within the polyamorous spectrum.

STRUCTURES AND FORMATIONS

1) Macro structures

Chosen family: In place of what is commonly understood as 'family', created either through birth or marriage, a chosen family is created with people who are selected based on shared ideas of life and values. Chosen families give both emotional and infrastructural support.

Polycule: A group or network of interconnected polyamorous relationships where various people may share various kinds of relationships with each other. An 'open' polycule allows for entry of new people into this network, whereas a 'closed' polycule does not. A closed polycule is also called a polyfidelitous group, often shortened to 'polify', which refers to the promise of fidelity within the group.

Poly family: This is a number of polyamorous people who may or may not live together, considering each other part of a family and taking on the roles and responsibilities of conventional families for each other.

2) Micro structures

Solo poly: A polyamorous person who prefers an independent and single life without sharing domesticity, finances, or child-rearing with any specific partner.

Dyad: The distinct relationship that two people have with each other in the larger polyamorous setting.

Triad: A polyamorous relationship of three people, all of whom are romantically and/or sexually involved with one another. This is often called a 'throuple'.

V: This is another kind of polyamorous relationship with three people, but here, like the letter V, only one person is romantically and/or sexually involved with two partners, but those partners don't share a relationship with each other.

Quad: A polyamorous relationship of four people connected with each other through romantic, sexual, or both kinds of involvements. It can start with a couple wanting more people in their lives, or two couples getting together.

N: Four people in a polyamorous setting are connected romantically and/or sexually with each other like the four points of the letter N. It is sometimes called a Z too.

Mono–poly: A relationship between a monoamorous person and a polyamorous person.

IDENTITY

1) Gender identity

Cisgender: Someone who identifies with the gender assigned at birth.

Transgender: Someone who identifies with a gender other than what was assigned at birth. Some use this generic term while others prefer to use 'trans man' or 'trans woman', depending on their self-identified preferred gender. I have also learnt from people much younger than me that 'trans masc' and 'trans fem' are terms used to identify with trans people who see themselves as either masculine or feminine, but do not want to associate with the words 'man' or 'woman'.

Genderqueer: Someone who identifies outside of the binaries of male and female and positions themselves somewhere on the gender spectrum. They can also be called 'agender' or 'non-binary'. They sometimes call themselves 'enby'.

2) Sexual identity

Asexual: Someone with very little or no sexual desire, interest, or attraction. They are also called 'ace'.

Heterosexual: Someone who is sexually attracted to the opposite binary gender identity. Here, it is important to note the term 'heteronormative', referring to the assumption that the social roles of heterosexual relationships is the only norm and that biological sex, gender identity, and gender roles are all the same.

Homosexual: Someone who is sexually attracted to people of their own gender identity.

Bisexual: Someone who is sexually attracted to people of their own gender identity as well as those of the opposite binary gender identity.

Polysexual: Someone who is sexually attracted to people of many but not all gender identities.

Pansexual: Someone who is sexually attracted to people of all gender identities.

Demisexual: Someone who generally falls in the asexual spectrum, but can feel sexual towards those with whom they can build solid emotional connection.

3) Romantic identity

Aromantic: Someone with very little or no romantic desire, interest, or attraction. They are also called 'aro'.

Demiromantic: Someone who generally falls in the aromantic spectrum but can feel romantic towards those with whom they can build solid emotional connection.

PRACTICES

1) Practices based on relationships between polyamorous people

Parallel polyamory: Here, each partner has multiple relationships but they are not connected to each other's partners in any way.

Kitchen-table polyamory: Here, a set of polyamorous people actively build close relationships of friendship, romance, and/or sexuality with each other's partners. The idea behind the name is that it is possible for all of them to share a meal on the kitchen table. A more intense form of this is sometimes called 'lap-sitting polyamory'.

Garden-party polyamory: In this practice, people in the relationship can choose to connect or not with each other's partners.

2) Practices based on prioritization of partners

Hierarchical relationships: Some partners are given priority over the others and have more power in setting rules and boundaries. However, priorities, over time, can shift between partners.

Non-hierarchical relationships: These are partnerships that attempt to create a more equal space with equal powers and intensity of relationships.

Relationship anarchy: This practice is a more intense form of non-hierarchical relationship, which enables a person to freely, spontaneously, and independently engage in various partnerships, without the responsibilities towards one limiting the engagements with another. People who follow this are called RA in short.

ROLES

Life partner: A romantic and/or sexual partner with whom there is a long-term committed relationship, hopefully for life.

Platonic life partner: A life partner with whom there is no romantic or sexual relationship but with whom one shares a deep bond and commitment to share life's responsibilities, which could include child-rearing.

Nesting partner: Often also called a domestic partner, this is someone with whom the home is shared and lived in.

Primary and secondary partners: Within a hierarchical polyamorous structure, the partner who has the most priority is the primary partner, while others are termed secondary. The primary partner may or may not be a nesting partner. There are cases where there may be more than one primary partner.

Anchor partner: In a non-hierarchical polyamorous structure, this is a partner who is seen as more dependable or trusted than others, with whom there is a longer and closer relationship. There may also be finance-sharing or home-sharing with them.

Comet: A relationship where partners don't have a continuous, intense everyday connection and may live far away from each other. Their relationship is played out when they meet every once in a while. This is similar to a comet that crosses paths with Earth at intervals.

Cowboy/Cowgirl: This is a person who may be monoamorous, pretending to be polyamorous and attempting to build a relationship with a polyamorous person only to pull them away from their other partners and convert them to monoamory. Cowpoke is also used as a gender-neutral word.

Hinge: A partner who is shared between two people. Like in a V or N situation.

Pivot: This is similar to a hinge, but there is one person who has many partners.

Metamour: A partner's partner, also called 'meta' for short.

Other significant other: This is an important partner who is not the primary partner.

Telemour: This is the partner of a metamour, who is not connected to the chosen polyamorous structure in any other way.

Unicorn: A woman who is willing to have a relationship with both members of a heterosexual couple. The name comes with reference to how rare they are. Couples who look out for unicorns are called unicorn-hunters.

Pegasus: A male version of the unicorn.

OTHER TERMS

Cheating: Like in monoamory, there is cheating in polyamory. It means violating any of the mutually agreed upon rules and terms of engagement set in a relationship.

Compersion: This is one of the pillars of polyamory and one of the most difficult practices. It means feeling joy when a partner receives happiness from being in another romantic and/or sexual relationship. It is the opposite of jealousy.

Frubble and wibble: While frubble denotes moments of compersion, wibble is a fleeting moment of insecurity or fear when seeing a partner being intimate or showing affection towards another person.

Don't ask, don't tell: Some relationships in polyamory maintain a strict code of silence on each other's relationships. This could happen in a very severe parallel polyamory.

Couple privilege: Sometimes, a couple could become the centre of a relationship hierarchy due to certain external factors like social structures or presumptions made by the people involved. This leads to the couple receiving undue privileges which may be unfair for the others.

Established-relationship energy: This is a cosy, secure, comfortable, and trusting feeling within a relationship that has continued for a while and seen many ups and downs. This used to be called old-relationship energy earlier.

New-relationship energy: This encapsulates the elation, buzz, and frenzy that come with a new relationship at its early stages.

Fluid bonding: When partners do not use barriers for sex and allow exchange of fluids. Polyamorous people often decide on the boundaries of fluid-bonding to limit the risk of unsafe sex.

One-penis policy: This is a situation where, in a polyamorous structure, only one person with a penis is allowed. This means that typically, a cis man is allowed multiple cis female partners who can each have relationships with other cis female partners only. Some consider it a transphobic policy as it denies entry to trans women and trans men.

Polysaturated: This is a person who is polyamorous but not currently open to new relationships.

Relationship escalator: This is the assumed normal trajectory of a typical heteronormative monogamous relationship which starts with dating, then living together, then marriage, and finally, having children.

Swinging: This is a practice that allows for engagement with sexual partners outside of an existing romantic partnership, with the caveat that it will be only sexual and not emotional or romantic. Couples engage in this in an organized manner.

Veto: This is a mutually agreed upon power given to a primary partner to terminate or restrict other relationships.

One might ask the purpose of so many new words, such complex terms, and the practice of speaking in ways that are alien, far removed from the way we are conditioned to speak about love and relationships. One may also wonder the purpose of naming everything—assigning words for every relationship, act, feeling, and practice. These questions have to be seen in the light of how the dominant narratives of monoamory and monogamy control the language of love.

Words grew around the practice of monoamory, through the conversations of everyday life as well as the arts of languages, including poetry, stories, and songs. Polyamory lived in the darkness of silence, or through secrets and codes. Therefore, creating words for polyamory that are unabashed and visible is a political act, just like the assertion of one's identity. However, one should not get lost in the sea of words but stay with their spirit and glean their meanings. The idea is to be able to use them to express our desires and their manifestations as fascinatingly as possible, breaking out of the bondage of the language of monoamory.

It is true that while words have great power to give shape to thoughts and make them tangible, they are also limiting. Once a word is created, it defines the thought, setting the boundary of its meaning. The easy fluidity, the nuanced ambiguity, the blurriness of imagined possibilities of polyamory could be lost in the sharp, chiselled body of the word. And there the fixedness of language could become the prison of polyamory. What irony that would be! This is something to keep in mind. Also, if a language becomes complicated, people may lose their use for it. The world has lost many languages to their inability to transform with life's many changes. A language needs to be as alive, nimble, flexible, and vibrant as the lives that produce it. It requires that gentleness of touch. The language of polyamory will also thrive when it dances the tango with the lived experiences that give birth to it.

16

BOAT OF HOPE V
'JEALOUSY IS A PART OF CONDITIONING'

Malathi (name changed) is in the legal profession and lives across multiple cities. She is in her early thirties. Vivek is a management consultant and lives in Bengaluru. He is in his early forties. They are in a polyamorous relationship where Malathi has another partner to whom she is married, and keeps a home with their pets. While Malathi and her married partner have been practising polyamory for some years, Vivek started exploring it for the first time over the past couple of years. I had the privilege of a conversation with both Malathi and Vivek separately, where they shared their lived experiences with me. I wanted to see the contours of their relationships and their larger engagement with polyamory from two different perspectives. Throughout these conversations, we were aware that the third voice—that of Malathi's married partner—was missing. I hope we have made enough space for the presence of that absence in our musings.

Malathi

Malathi has been openly polyamorous for many years now. While in Bengaluru, she divides her time between her married partner and Vivek. She has other significant relationships in her life, too. She is an active member of polyamorous support groups and advises and advocates on various issues.

(A. G.: Arundhati Ghosh / M: Malathi)

ON DISCOVERING POLYAMORY

A. G.: How did you discover polyamory?

M: I've always had a problem with monogamy, ever since my teen years. The idea that I could only love one person and that sex was limited to one person for the rest of my life didn't sit well with me. As a woman, monogamy felt like ownership over my mind and body, and I didn't like that. I think I first articulated this to my brother when I was seventeen or eighteen. I discovered the term 'polyamory' only in my twenties. But, by then, I had already been in a series of failed monogamous relationships because I realized that I was unable to stop myself from having feelings for people who were not my partners.

A. G.: Where are you with your polyamorous life today?

M: Today, I'm married to one person and I'm also with other people. We opened up our marriage in the early years by doing away with sexual fidelity, but this was not just random sex that we were having. Rather, these were meaningful and fulfilling connections that meant something to each of us. More often than not, we have had connections with the same person and together. That's my marriage and it's been beautiful.

I am also in very rewarding relationships with Vivek and others. Vivek and I met on Bumble more than a year ago. We've just hit it off really well. I am grateful he and my other partners are in my life.

A. G.: What does being polyamorous mean for you?

M: One way to put it is that I get to love more. But, another way to see it is that I am taking control of my feelings, my autonomy, and myself overall. The way I see it, I'm owning my space through polyamory. If I fuck up along the way, I learn and grow from that experience. I guess, for me, it's about self-discovery and trying to be a better and more sensitive person. Having different people in my life opens my eyes to perspectives I wouldn't have seen if I was not polyamorous.

ON BUILDING RELATIONSHIPS

A. G.: What kind of rules, negotiations, or discussions do you get into in a relationship?

M: The first thing is setting up personal boundaries. It takes a lot of time to figure out what one is comfortable with, and this is a deeply personal journey that requires us to hold up the mirror to ourselves. Identifying boundaries is a constant thing, because they may shift, change, or even disappear over time, depending on how one grows.

Time is probably the biggest topic of negotiation. I think this is a constant thing with most poly people. But, somewhere, feeling grateful for the amount of time I have with all my partners and the fact that they want to spend that time with me is helpful.

I think rules can cover many things. Open communication and honesty are important, especially when one starts seeing someone new. Living arrangements, finances, domestic stuff also become open to negotiations and discussions, especially with nesting partners.

A. G.: What do loyalty and security mean for you in polyamory?

M: I think loyalty comes with how well you respect your partner and their boundaries. It includes how one safeguards partners through their likes and boundaries, and how one works from a 'best interest' perspective. Like, asking myself the question, am I acting in their best interest? Often this also means clarifying with them whether a choice I made is okay with them.

I don't think we can attach the word 'security' in the way it's thought of by the monogamous world, to polyamorous situations. It is not about stability or longevity. That is a disclaimer before I proceed. Security in polyamorous contexts is a reflection on how one feels secure about themself in the first place before attaching notions of security to the relationship itself. This may be true for monogamy too, but it doesn't get discussed as much. We tend to be reluctant to address our insecurities with partners in any kind of relationship setting because we've been beaten into this thinking that a 'strong' person is someone with no insecurities. Nobody is like that. Talking about what makes us feel insecure, recognizing that insecurities are not stagnant and can change with different partners is important. But, perhaps, the most important thing is finding the confidence to say, 'I'm feeling insecure.' And maybe, being able to say that in a relationship is security!

A. G.: What is the role of honesty and consent in your relationships?

M: Consent is super important. But, whether we view consent as veto power or a constant ongoing discussion is important. Sometimes, it should operate as a veto; other times it probably operates in a more shifty space—like I started out consenting to the situation, but now I'm having second thoughts. That doubt, while disruptive, can be good to identify discomfort or insecurities. I don't think consent is a one-way street. It operates in a more dynamic manner where everyone involved is confronted with a situation.

Honesty is key to sustaining any relationship. But the question, really, is whether we are being honest with ourselves about our feelings towards a situation or a person. You can have all the open communication you want, but it won't really be 'open' if you're not able to figure out what you're truly thinking or feeling and why. I think this is where I struggle—identifying how I'm feeling. So, honesty is not just about telling the truth, but also about discovering yourself.

ON JEALOUSY AND CO-LOVING

A. G.: How do you handle jealousy and possessiveness?

M: I started very early on, not wanting to be anybody's 'possession'. I apply the same standard to my partners; they are not my possessions. We possess material stuff, not people. As a feminist, this was my biggest problem with monogamy. It brings people down to possessions—the 'you are mine' or 'my girl' (though that's a nice song, I hate the lyrics) sort of talk. I think this is particularly damaging. So, I haven't had this problem since I was a teenager. The bigger issue here is how I'm affected by someone's actions, or how my actions affect the other person. And that's the dynamic one has to figure out.

Jealousy is a part of conditioning in my opinion. But, it is a helpful feeling because it allows us to identify what we're feeling insecure or unsure about. Many times, it is because I am probably moralizing a situation or my own feelings. Or that I feel inadequate. So, one way of working through this is to seek out that adequacy in myself. Sometimes, just telling myself 'I'm enough' is okay, and at other times, I may need a bit of a push from my partners. I don't think polyamorous people are alone in this struggle.

A. G.: *What kind of relationships do you have with your co-lovers or metamours?*

M: Well, my metamour (my married partner's other partner) and I do have contact; it is not a friendship yet, but hopefully it will evolve into that one day. I really appreciate her and am grateful that she is in his life because she helps him grow as a person. We took a very long time to meet, but then when we did, we hit it off really well. I am just so happy she's around and it makes me feel supported that he has her support. I hope to meet my other metamours someday. But some of them are monoamorous and may find it overwhelming to meet me, and that's okay.

A. G.: *Do you have hierarchies in your relationships? Between your married partner and Vivek specifically, how do you maintain balance? What does that mean for all three of you?*

M: This is a tough question because I personally don't subscribe to hierarchical polyamory, but both my married partner and Vivek consider me as their primary. That gets a little tricky sometimes. Not for any other reason but my own beliefs about non-hierarchical polyamory.

I usually nest with my married partner. Vivek and I were trying to set up a co-living situation too, where I would spend a few days a week with him. My married partner also has another partner and I really want him to spend time with her too, because I see how much that relationship means to him. I think we are currently winging it on some level because we don't have a set schedule. Plus, now I live away from the city where my married partner and Vivek live, for about eight months a year. It feels overwhelming to think of bringing about a balance sometimes. Sometimes, I wonder if it works like a time-share also because of the multiple demands that are placed on me with work, family, friends, self-care, and other stuff. But, I do think that somehow we do end up in a balanced situation because I get to spend time at home with my married partner and our dogs, and meet other partners. Limited time is the bane of my life.

ON STRUGGLES

A. G.: What do you continue to struggle with?

M: I think the biggest struggle for me is the fact that I cannot be openly polyamorous as a married person. It sucks because I feel like I have to hide my other partners from my world—like my family. It's just not fair to everyone involved and staying hidden is not a nice feeling. If someone has a privacy concern and they don't want to come out, that's fine. But, as a norm, it feels like poly people live underground because of how precarious it can get for us if we're outed. And that kind of vulnerability is a constant struggle. I am constantly afraid of what can happen if I'm outed.

I currently live in Haryana where I'm working; (it's) not exactly the best place for a poly woman. What if I lose my job because people at work moralize against it? What if my parents, with whom I have a loving relationship, stop talking to me over this? What if I'm kicked out of my rented house because neighbours discover I'm poly and complain to the owner? The list of 'what ifs' is endless. It also eats away at any confidence one may have on coming out as poly.

I think the level of vulnerability for me as a queer woman is also higher as compared to my partners who are cis men. Dating apps are a constant struggle because these are fairly violent spaces for vulnerable people. My profile says 'happily married and polyamorous', but the number of times men have matched with me on dating apps just to say violent stuff to me because my profile is honest still amazes me. The number of men who refuse to look at me beyond just being another 'lay' really sucks. Women or people who identify as other genders won't engage with me because I'm married.

As women and queer people in India, we are constantly worried about sexual violence too. Being a queer poly woman feels like I'm doubly vulnerable. These are very palpable fears. My partners and I are constantly on the lookout for red flags. It can get exhausting at times and my reaction has been to just delete dating apps altogether for long periods after a negative experience. It takes a while to feel like I'm ready to get back on them.

Vivek

Vivek has lived across many countries, imbibing various cultures. He was once married for about five years, and had been monoamorous for most of his life. His entry into this world of polyamory has been recent and brings with it many questions, doubts, and experiments. In his conversation with me, he responded from the context of being in this V formation of a relationship with Malathi, as well as his own thoughts on exploring polyamory.

(A. G.: Arundhati Ghosh / V: Vivek)

ON DISCOVERING POLYAMORY

AG: How did you discover polyamory?
V: I am someone who has, almost his entire life, been monoamorous and believed in 'happily ever after' relationships which lead to marriage. I discovered polyamory about a year ago when I met Malathi on Bumble. As we discussed polyamory, I was honestly very confused and my mind was filled with multiple questions. 'Is this just another new-fangled millennial construct for having sex with multiple people, sans emotions or commitment?' 'Can this really work out for me?' 'Will I honestly get quality time with her, when I want it?' 'Am I setting myself up for heartbreak by

believing in the "amory" part of polyamory?' And so on and so forth. I am happy to affirm today, hand on heart, that polyamory is one of the best things to have ever happened to me.

A. G.: *Share with us how this journey has been for you over the past year or so with your partners?*

V: The past one year has been a very eventful and fulfilling journey for me. I have clarified a lot of my misconceptions. I have been reading up and discussing what it really means to be polyamorous. I have spent quality time with Malathi. We have often had differing points of view, but have been able to discuss them rationally and constructively (as in any healthy relationship). I am today much deeper in love with and much more emotionally attached to Malathi than I ever imagined I could have been a year ago.

While currently I am in a relationship with only Malathi, I completely subscribe to polyamory! I recently met someone whom I've been seeing a lot, and we are discussing about us being in a polyamorous relationship. I do realize it's a binary outcome where we may be partners or not, once the new-relationship energy settles and we get to know each other more intimately. However, what simply boggles my mind is—I can openly explore a relationship with other people, and not compromise my relationship with my primary partner Malathi. This is truly a very beautiful thing.

A. G.: *What does being polyamorous mean for you?*

V: Most importantly, I no longer need to hide, or have guilt about feeling attracted to or wanting to be with someone who isn't my primary partner. I can explore different interests with different partners, and do not need to compromise or limit what I want to do based upon my primary partner's interests. For example, my primary partner enjoys diverse food experiences like me but prefers to stay at home and not travel. Today, I no longer have to grumble and negotiate with her to please join me in these activities. Nor do I need to deny myself those experiences, and build up unhappiness or resentment. I can search for, and hope that I discover another partner with whom I may enjoy my interests, or potentially develop new interests. Of course, there is no playbook or guarantees here that the stars will align oh-so-perfectly but hey, isn't it nice to have the possibility? I am now able to share and provide a lot more love, and receive a lot more love, than I ever could in a monoamorous construct. If I had to summarize my thoughts and emotions, I would simply state that I feel free and happy.

ON BUILDING RELATIONSHIPS

A. G.: What kind of rules, negotiations, or discussion did you have when you began this journey with your relationship?

V: The most important rule which Malathi and I practise is being brutally honest and transparent about everything—who we date, who we fuck, who we secretly love or lust for, our thoughts and emotions and feelings. I have learned during my relationship with Malathi to unlearn and forget a lot of my past baggage with respect to trust issues, and be completely and beautifully bare. I find that extremely refreshing and liberating!

Some important boundaries we have discussed and agreed on are that I do not criticize/speak deprecatingly about her other partners, or expect all of her available time and mind-space as I may have expected in a monoamorous set-up.

A. G.: What do loyalty and security mean for you in polyamory?

V: At first brush, loyalty and security do appear to be all-weather values. However, these are very different animals in monoamorous and polyamorous relationships.

Conventional monoamory considers physical intimacy as the Holy Grail for discerning loyalty in relationships. Personally, I do not put sex on a pedestal. I see all humans as creatures of desire, who are fundamentally incapable of monoamorous behaviours. I do not consider the occasional hook-up as justifiable cause to erode my trust or respect for my partner. What would have been unacceptable for me is for my partner to have developed emotions for another man, even if they've never grazed fingers. Let's now juxtapose this with my ex-partner considering me to be a disloyal cheating bastard if I so much as fantasized about any other person.

Porn included. Looking at other girls for over five seconds was punishable with sex being withheld for weeks. And drama. I had never felt as suffocated in my life.

Now, let's discuss about me and Malathi. An episode from *Two and a Half Men* comes to mind—'A Lungful of Alan'. Malathi, the love of my life, is just that to me. A freaking big breath of fresh air. For us, loyalty and security mean telling each other about all the dumb muppet crap we did all week, and receiving zero judgement. Comfort and security for us mean cooking a meal and feeding each other, or giving each other a massage. Or just a big bear hug, and saying we love each other.

A. G.: What is the role of honesty and consent in your relationships?

V: I see honesty as being exponentially important in polyamory as a polyamorous lifestyle does not provide us with licences for wilful behaviour. Our loved ones continue to be individuals with feelings, insecurities, and baggage.

Hypothetical examples: 1) Your partner(s) are big beautiful people and they cannot comprehend why you are partnering with an athletic person, 2) Your partner(s) are nice wonderful awesome doggo peeps...and for some inexplicable reason, you choose to date someone who likes felines. Obviously, your partner(s) will be like 'what the fuck'—was anything you ever told me real?! So yeah, it is very important to openly discuss your dating choices with your partner(s), and find a harmonious solution which works for everyone.

With us, Malathi prefers that I inform her whenever I date someone, whereas I am comfortable with her waiting till she has fallen in love, and sees them as a potential partner. However, being honest does *not* mean us sharing intimate details of what was done or said with others. So yeah, we have defined what honesty means for us, and what it does not. And neither of us has developed a Pinocchio nose over the last year.

ON JEALOUSY AND CO-LOVING

A. G.: How do you handle jealousy and possessiveness?

V: I do not feel jealous about Malathi having other partners or lovers. I have always been very aware of my charms, my strengths, and shortcomings. I am aware of why she chose me as a partner in her life. Hence, I feel very secure in our relationship.

I have, on occasion, been jealous of her having spent more time with another partner or how she may have spoken about another partner. However, for us, the silver bullet has been honesty. I've been able to speak with her about how I feel and why, and we have been able to address it in a mutually amicable manner.

Regarding possession, can one really possess or own another person? Hell no! Do I wish Malathi could be with me all the time? While I do love her to bits, this isn't something which either of us wants (so we can explore our respective polyamorous lifestyles), nor would it be healthy for our relationship.

A. G.: What kind of relationships do you have with your co-lover(s)?

V: I have once hung out with her married partner when I stayed over at Malathi and his home. We had a nice evening and lots of interesting discussions over drinks and dinner but then it became a bit awkward for me. Would Malathi go to his room or mine? May I ask Malathi to come cuddle with me at night? Earlier that day, I had asked her about the social protocols involved when hanging out with a co-lover. Her guidance: 'Boo face, just be the way you normally are.'

Equipped with that wonderful clarity, I texted Malathi and asked if it would be kosher for her to spend the night with me. As I did not receive her reply, yours truly wished them good night and went to sleep with the constant company of mosquitoes. As we had our morning coffee and smoke, Malathi started giggling wildly and said, 'Aiyyo Boo! I is so sorry, I just saw your message.' After an animated exchange, which isn't print-worthy, I learnt that I could have simply asked. Oh well, you live and you learn, right? On the whole, my relationship and interactions with my co-lover have been amicable, sans any awkwardness.

A. G.: Do you have hierarchies in your relationships?

V: I consider my relationship with Malathi as my primary relationship. She is the most important and valuable person to me in my romantic relationships, and will continue to be. What this means practically is that I do not make dating or relationship choices sans her consent/being on board with my choices.

ON STRUGGLES

A. G.: What are some of the most difficult parts of this journey?

V: Simply put, it has been sharing Malathi's available time and mind-space with her other partners. More importantly, it has been about me not being able to scream from the rooftops about having this incredible life partner as societies do not yet have the understanding or acceptance of polyamory as a lifestyle. Another work in progress for me is fully accepting that Malathi cannot live exclusively with me whenever she is living in Bengaluru.

A. G.: Polyamorous people are seen as shallow, fickle, and often amoral—any responses?

V: Based on my limited knowledge and understanding of polyamorous persons (given that I have only interacted and discussed with Malathi) and my independent reflections, I will say this: I definitely believe that a polyamorous lifestyle is a moral lifestyle choice—it is honest, open, and transparent. And as all things in life are, it is a choice. If it does not work for you, then you need to reconsider your life choices.

A. G.: Have you come out as a polyamorous person to anyone— friends, family? How did they react?

V: Yes, I came out last year to my brother and sister-in-law about me being in a polyamorous relationship with Malathi. They discounted it as me just wanting to get laid/being confused/trying to keep up with the younger people. This was disappointing as I expected them to be more understanding.

I also came out to my mother a month ago. Her concerns were more centred on me contracting unwanted STDs/STIs due to this 'promiscuous' lifestyle (and thankfully, less about me not providing her with grandchildren, ha ha!). However, what I do appreciate a lot about my conversations with my mother is that they are mature and not dramatic. I presented my point of view to my mother—that I believe dating a polyamorous/ethical non-monogamous person is way safer than dating a person pretending to be monoamorous but clandestinely sleeping around.

While the jury is still out on this, I am cautiously optimistic that my mother will someday understand and accept my choice to be in a polyamorous lifestyle.

A. G.: Do you ever doubt yourself and want to be monoamorous again? Where do these doubts take you? How do you resolve them?

V: Yes, I have had doubts, and still do question whether I may want to resume a monoamorous lifestyle. The root cause of my doubt is my desire (albeit waning, with age) to have a biological child. I know that I cannot have a biological child with Malathi, and that it is unlikely that a future poly partner may be interested in having a biological child with me. My utopian wish is to meet a poly girl who is happy to have a biological child with me.

What does bother me the most about these doubts is the prospect of no longer having Malathi in my life. Which I find extremely hard to digest. What I can say today with certainty is this—I may choose to practise monoamory in the future, if utopia (or a semblance of it) does not present itself. However, I will always believe that polyamory is the right choice for the person I am.

A. G.: As a once-married and divorced person, what has being polyamorous opened up for you?

V: Being divorced is never easy. It is incrementally harder when you need to heal from an emotionally and/or physically abusive marriage. You need to unlearn and forget the unhealthy stuff, and re-discover intimacy and love. A year or so after my divorce, my parents gently suggested, 'Would you like to re-marry?' I would always dodge the question as I had so many doubts—did the right person really exist? Would I be able to make it work? Would I get divorced again, with new scars and trauma? It was terrifying.

I had started dating shortly after my divorce. I consciously sought out people who wanted to date casually. It felt light and comfortable. Rejection, or discontinuation at some point, was not emotionally hard as there was no real, tangible loss. I did not have to worry about being asked, 'Where do you see this going?' This idyllic phase of casual dating ended. I began to feel unfulfilled and incomplete, and wanted a loving, healthy, and long-term relationship. However, I did not know what a safe way to seek this was.

It was during this confusing period that Malathi and I met. As we grew closer and more comfortable in our relationship, I was able to discard the masks I had developed after my divorce. In her, I found my safe and happy space.

WADING IN, SAILING ALONG: CONTINUING WITH LIVES LOVES DIFFERENTLY

I see different kinds of people in love around me. Most are monoamorous couples. They are like couples generally are—happy, sad, struggling, living with the fragility of being human. Many among them have had relationships outside of their couple-hoods, known or unknown to their partners; have lived in denial with, or been accepted by their partners. I have always found it hard to be judgemental about the intricate workings of relationships or their outcomes. Each is so different from another that it is difficult to attempt to stretch their messy layers across the same frameworks of ethics, or codify and categorize their virtues and vices. What is sacred, what is honest, what is shared, what is denied—are all defined, understood, and manifested differently by different folks. Life is complex, and being polyamorous, I understand deeply the needs of the body and the soul, whether or not permission for their satiation is presently available in society. As long as there is consent and equity of power—all else is a matter of adjustment.

But what this also tells me is that monoamory is neither infallible nor a recipe for success in and of itself, whatever way we may want to define it in our relationships. If the desire so calls for, why not leave the shore behind and wade in to discover the ocean, albeit on experimental boats and home-made sails? Swimming against the tide does require more power, more resilience, and sometimes more trust in one's beliefs. While the practice of polyamory tests all of the above, it is also said that swimming against the tide for a while makes you realize you have developed muscles you did not even know you had!

Some of my friends are 'polyskeptics'. They wonder if this will ever work; they find faults with how we hesitate to provide clear answers to all their trick questions. Their enquiries consist of many ifs, buts, and howevers. What I attempt to tell them is that from certain angles, nothing works! Life is so much about giving things a try, attempting to do, desiring to be. There is no certainty in any of the options that relationships of love present before us. So, if some people want to play around with the rules in order to open up different possibilities of loving and living, what's the harm in it? After all, they also bear the consequences of these explorations. If I am not feeling very charitable towards these friends, I pin their cynicism on their own inability to find happiness in love, or to come to terms with the dissatisfaction of emotional upheavals in their lives. But on most days, I understand how terrifying and lonely it is when love does not work out quite how we were promised it would.

People ask me if polyamory has made me happy and content. And I say yes—emphatically. It has also made me brave, expansive, replete. Has it made me sad and despondent, I am asked too. Yes, many times. Like all love, this comes with its trials by fire, tests by flood. I have been both burnt and drowned. There is no difference here between monoamory and polyamory. Love has the power to break us. To love is also to know that we might be witness to our own cracking. But then, the broken are the really brave, because they embody proof of encounter with something larger, stronger, and more powerful than themselves. They bear evidence of having lived through that and survived. Like Akhilandeshwari, the goddess who is 'never not broken', it is in this brokenness that we witness our truths, and undertake journeys to continuously recreate ourselves.

But don't I want to 'settle down'? Ma, although accepting of my choice and approving of my partners, or 'bondhu' (friend in Bangla) as she likes to call them, still worries sometimes about the lack of a singular and permanent companion in my life. I laugh and tell her she just needs a single person to whom she may complain about me and multiple people just confuse her. More seriously, most people will tell you this settling down is the ultimate destination of life. However, in my case, and with many other polyamorous folks as well—we rejoice in our journeys with many loves, make stopovers as we go along, and don't think much of final destinations. After all, the twelfth-century poet, philosopher, saint, and activist of my home state Karnataka, Basavanna had revealed:

> *Listen, O lord of the meeting rivers,*
> *things standing shall fall,*
> *but the moving ever shall stay*

—translated from the Kannada by A. K. Ramanujan

There was a time when I looked to define love—narrowing its scope and focus, increasing the sharpness of light on it, tightly articulating it within heavily guarded boundaries. Ordering it to raise its hand and distinguish itself from other relationships, I did not hesitate to make love a lonesome only child with all expectations of my dreams on its weary shoulders.

Attempting to create a spill-free environment, I made sure that the 'line of control' around love was strongly adhered to with strict embargos on strays. There was no space for ifs and maybes, no room for ambiguity. But today, with all my greys, I look at love as a gentler blur. Overflowing and swirling in its porousness, it negotiates barbed fences and erases borders between romance, friendship, and family. When I speak to many of my polyamorous friends, I realize they feel the same way. The conditioned definitions of love melt away into wholesome care, quiet compassion, and deeper responsibilities. Definitions don't matter anymore. I touch my heart and I know that life is richer when love and land are kinder to refugees. And that another world is being lived right here, right now, with all our loves.

FURTHER EXPLORATIONS: MY TOP TEN RESOURCES ON POLYAMORY

There are many books, podcasts, and other resources available online for those desiring to explore polyamory. The range includes material on conceptual frameworks, practical advice, workbooks, real-life case studies as well as fictional accounts. What I am sharing here is a list of my personal top-ten resources that, over the past many years, helped me get a better sense of the world of love, relationships, and polyamory. I hope you enjoy them as much as I did.

1. *The Ethical Slut (Third Edition): A Practical Guide to Polyamory, Open Relationships and Other Freedoms in Sex and Love* by Janet W. Hardy and Dossie Easton

   The first edition of this book opened my eyes. Now the enriched and rejuvenated third edition is here. Based on how to build ethical non-monogamous relationships, it is a wonderful journey into understanding the joys and hardships that are encountered. It has helpful tips, exercises, and several examples from life to illustrate the practical advice and suggestions.

2. *All About Love: New Visions* by bell hooks

   A perfect combination of practical sensibility and philosophical wisdom, this book challenges conventional notions of love and enables fresh perspectives. Exploring love through the varied lenses of gender, race, and class, it helps self-reflection and creating healthy relationships with others. Though not on polyamory, this book has been a primer for me to understand love.

3. *When Someone You Love Is Polyamorous: Understanding Poly People and Relationships* by Dr Elisabeth Scheff

This is a short pamphlet for beginners with basic and accessible facts as an introduction to polyamory. It gives clear conceptual understanding, addresses misconception, and offers practical suggestions with real-life examples. With focused information, it does not overwhelm the reader with too many details. This was one of the first materials I read on polyamory.

4. *Intimate Relations: Exploring Indian Sexuality* by Sudhir Kakar

This is considered a significant work in understanding sexuality and relationships in India from a psychoanalytical perspective. It addresses how history, social structures, and cultural practices influence intimate relationships in India. While this is a much-debated book, for me, it offered a deep dive into the Indian psyche. It was a pleasurable book to read due to the mythological and literary references as well.

5. *The Jealousy Workbook: Exercises and Insights for Managing Open Relationships* by Kathy Labriola

Empathetic and non-judgemental, this book enables developing various kinds of emotional and intellectual skills to nurture healthy relationships. It is a fabulous self-help guidebook that has various exercises to cope with jealousy, which is seen as a natural emotion.

6. *Many Love: A Memoir of Polyamory and Finding Love(s)* by Sophie Lucido Johnson

This is an autobiographical graphic novel that is funny, feminist, and fast-paced. It gently narrates the story of polyamorous lives with humour and charm. While it examines conventional structures of love and its demands, it is both compassionate and courageous in suggesting alternative possibilities of being.

7. *Polysecure: Attachment, Trauma and Consensual Nonmonogamy* by Jessica Fern

Written from healing and therapeutic perspectives, this book guides polyamorous relationships through the intersections of psychological needs and an ethical framework. It uses the attachment theory to address wounds caused in relationships and focuses on self-work and reflection through which to build the skills and capacity to navigate challenges. This book is for a slightly more evolved reader who may be already practising polyamory.

8. *Love's Not Color Blind: Race and Representation in Polyamorous and Other Alternative Communities* by Kevin A. Patterson

This is a collection of first-person perspectives on the intersection of race, sexuality, and relationship structures within alternative communities. Focusing on inclusivity and safety, this book is for those interested in a deeper understanding of intersectional identities and community-building. While reading this, I wondered what a similar book with the Dalit perspective in India could look like.

9. *Stepping off the Relationship Escalator: Uncommon Love and Life* by Amy Gahran

Over 1,500 people were interviewed in the making of this book that explores various ways of loving and living outside of monogamy. These include polyamory, swinging, and open relationships as well as living alone and non-prioritizing any one partner. It is written in a funny and practical manner.

10. *The Polyamory Breakup Book: Causes, Prevention, and Survival* by Kathy Labriola

This one is for those already in polyamorous relationships. It brings deep insights and empathetic advice for people to deal with difficult break-ups. It is practical and wise and has been my go-to book to understand why friendships and other relationships fail, especially when the reasons are embedded in uneven communication and difficulties in understanding each other's point of view.

THOSE WHO MADE THIS BOOK POSSIBLE

I discovered the pleasure of cooking very late in life. But the explorations in the kitchen very quickly alerted me to how appropriately the metaphor of making food could be wielded to illustrate the workings of various aspects of life. Writing this book is no exception. Cooking is seemingly a very solo and independent practice. But actually, when I want to cook and start looking at ingredients available at home, I am immediately connected to recipes I have read or heard that belonged to the lives and kitchens of other people, advice and warnings shared by those who have cooked this dish before me, and memories of me eating it at someone else's dining table. I remember incidents connected to the dish—a tinkle of laughter here, a satisfied belch there. Faces that I may not even remember vividly, gather around. Many whirling worlds tumble into my kitchen, adding their magic to my cooking, making it a collective expedition across generations. In the same way, writing, too, is seen as a solo journey. And yet, just like cooking, writing this book has been possible only because of the many people who have touched my life, sharing their time, stories, strength, and kindness with me.

Some of these people asked me difficult questions and pushed me to reconsider my interpretations. Others opened new strands of explorations by disagreeing with my premises. Still others held out mirrors whenever I seemed to stray from who I am. And then there were those who knew exactly when to buy me a whiskey and when to bring me a pillow. I would like to acknowledge each of their presence in the making of this book.

Kaushik Bhaduri, for his affection and showing me so early in life that there could be other ways to love.

Katrina Thompson, for being the oracle who foretold the making of this book.

Friends on Facebook, for discussing my polyamory posts with enthusiasm and truthfulness.

Sreemoyee Kundu, for inviting me to share my 'multiple' story in her book on single people.

Paromita Vohra, for starting Agents of Ishq to 'give sex a good name' and us the courage to speak of love without shame.

Debasmita Das and Varsha Ramachandran of the Agents of Ishq, for inviting me for my first public chat online on polyamory and holding space with such grace.

Barkha Kumari of *Deccan Herald*, for bravely inviting me to do a long article on polyamory in their Saturday special.

Chinki Sinha of *Outlook*, for her audacious decision to do an issue on alternative ways of loving and inviting me to write an article on polyamory.

Ravichandar, for having me on a panel to discuss polyamory during the International Women's Day celebrations at the Bangalore International Centre.

Priya Ramani, for holding that panel boldly together with chutzpah and humour.

Anna Thomas, for risking a chat on polyamory with me for Women Uninterrupted, The Hindu Podcast.

Shuddhabrata Sengupta, for the engaged conversation and witty repartees over the years.

Sumantra Ghosal, for being curious and listening even when he disagreed.

Bangalore Polycule and its members, for making space for a community whose love is still taboo.

Kaushik Bhaduri, Lea Christen, Shankar, Revathi, Subir, Mandeep Raikhy, Sidharth Sarkar, Kabir, Brijesh, Madham, Kalpi, Malathi, and Vivek, for trusting me with their journeys.

Arvind Narrain, for his constant encouragement to write this book and sharing his views on the legal aspects of polyamory.

Dolashree Mysoor, for her thoughtful contributions on the legal questions on polyamory.

Tamanna and Arulan P. S. Elai, for patiently responding to my questions on mental health.

Abhibyanjana Rubhi Thatal, for the rigorous research assistance on non-monogamous cultures.

Praggya Munshi, for believing in my efforts to understand the struggles of her generation.

Aditya Nigam, for painstakingly going through the manuscript.

Sumana Chadrashekar, for writing her book at the same time and sharing the work.

Kanishka Gupta of Writer's Side, for coming into my life like an angel and guiding my foray into publishing.

Soham of Writer's Side, for reading the manuscript with criticality and joy.

Aienla Ozukum of Aleph Book Company, for having faith in our journeys and trust in my telling.

Shaoni Sarkar, for helping me sculpt the book with her gentle nudges.

Bena Sareen, for making the beautiful cover all about our loves.

Ma, for making meanings of the stories I tell her.

Baba, for staying after leaving.

Aslambhai, Margaret, and Pia, for looking after home and hearth.

Clare Bayley and Chris Higgins, for being my home in London.

Lovers who parted ways, for unfinished hearts that left me sadder and wiser.

Co-lovers, for tests and testimonies with their presence and absence.

Mimi Munshi, Kaushik Bhaduri, Sandeep Menon, Gail Sinha, Samrat Som, Chris Higgins, Clare Bayley, Pankaj Singh, Menaka Rodriguez, Sarbari Dasgupta, Darshana Dave, Heba Hage Felder, Peter Jenkinson, Shelagh Wright, and Aditya Nigam (in the order that they appeared in my life)—for being the family chosen and woven over half a century.

Mimi Munshi, for allowing the past to yield its closed fist, sometimes.

Samrat Som, for the tentative being and charming impermanence.

Dadabhai, for never letting time feel like distance.

That One, for making my incredible dreams come true, and the worst nightmares too.

Sandeep Menon, for being my rock, having my back, and to my grateful dismay, never mincing words.

Aditya Nigam, for travelling along me in desire and vulnerability, with many loves, striving to be the promise.

SELECT BIBLIOGRAPHY

BOOKS

Alter, Robert, '*The Five Books of Moses: A Translation with Commentary*, New York: W.W. Norton & Co, 2004.

Beckermann, Stephen, and Lizarralde, Roberto, *The Ecology of the Barí: Rainforest Horticulturalists of Latin America*, Austin: University of Texas Press, 2013.

Brandon, Marianne, *Monogamy: The Untold Story*, Westport: Praeger (An imprint of Bloomsbury Publishing), 2010.

Dalal, Roshen, *Hinduism: An Alphabetical Guide*, New Delhi: Penguin India, 2010.

Engels, Frederick, *The Origin of the Family, Private Property and the State*, 1884.

Foster, Lawrence, 'Free Love and Community: John Humphrey Noyes and the Oneida Perfectionists', *America's Communal Utopias*, Donald E. Pitzer (ed.), The University of North Carolina Press, 1997.

Hill, Kim, and Hurtado, A. M., *Ache Life History: The Ecology and Demography of a Foraging People*, New York: Routledge (An imprint of Taylor & Francis Group), 1996.

Ramanujan, A. K. (tr.), *Speaking of Siva*, Harmondsworth: Penguin Books, 1973.

Reichard, Ulrich H., and Boesch, Christophe (eds.), *Monogamy: Mating Strategies and Partnerships in Birds, Humans and Other Mammals*, Cambridge: Cambridge University Press, 2003.

Thomas, Nicholas, 'Domestic Structures and Polyandry in the Marquesas Islands', *Family and Gender in the Pacific: Domestic contradictions and the colonial impact*, Margaret Jolly and Martha Macintyre (eds.), Cambridge: Cambridge University Press, 1989.

Vogel, Lise, *Marxism and the Oppression of Women: Toward a Unitary Theory*, New Brunswick: Rutgers University Press, 1983.

Washburn, Sherwood L., and Lancaster, G. S., 'The evolution of hunting', *Man the Hunter*, Richard B. Lee and Irven Devore (eds.), New York: Aldine De Gruyter, 1987.

Willey, Angela, *Undoing Monogamy: The Politics of Science and the Possibilities of Biology*, Durham: Duke University Press, 2016.

Zietzen, Miriam Koktvedgaard, *Polygamy a Cross-Cultural Analysis*, London: Routledge (An imprint of Taylor & Francis Group), 2008.

ARTICLES, ESSAYS, & OTHER SOURCES

Alger, Ingela, 'Monogamy: exception or rule?', Hal.science, 7 July 2020, available at https:// hal.science/hal-03097027v1.

Betzig, Laura, 'Roman Monogamy', Vol. 13, Issues 5-6, *Ethology and Sociobiology*, September–November 1992.

Cusack, Carole, 'Kerista: WRSP Profile' (2017), wrldrels.org, 15 January 2017, available at https://wrldrels.org/2017/01/19/kerista-commune/.

Dixon, Marlene, 'The Subjugation of Women Under Capitalism: The Bourgeois Morality', Vol. 1, No. 4, *Synthesis*, 1977.

Downey, Martha Elias, 'Monasticism, Monotheism, and Monogamy: Past and Present Expressions of the Undivided Life', Vol. 10, No. 8, *Religions*, 20 August 2019.

Goitsemodimo, Gosiame Amy, 'Modjadji- The Rain Queen', nationalmuseumpublications.co.za, 6 September 2019, available at https:// nationalmuseumpublications.co.za/modjadji-the-rain-queen/.

Gough, E. Kathleen, 'The Nayars and the Definition of Marriage', *The Journal of the Royal Anthropological Institute of Great Britain and Ireland*, Vol. 89, No. 1 (Jan.-Jun., 1959).

Komaja.org

Luintel, Youba Raj, 'Agency, autonomy and the shared sexuality: gender relations in polyandry in Nepal Himalaya', Vol. 31, No. 1, *Contributions to Nepalese Studies*, 1 January 2004.

Lukas, D., Clutton-Brock, T. H., 'The Evolution of Social Monogamy in Mammals', Vol. 341, No. 6145, *Science*, 2 August 2013.

MacDonald, Kevin, 'The Establishment and Maintenance of Socially Imposed Monogamy in Western Europe', Vol. 14, *Politics and the Life Sciences*, 1995.

Mukherji, Anahita, 'Hijra Farsi: Secret language knits community', *The Times of India*, 7 October 2013.

Nagarajan, Rema, 'Multiple wives most common among tribals: NFHS data', *The Times of India*, 28 July 2022.

'Oneida Community (1848-1880): A utopian community', socialwelfare.library. vcu.edu, 15 February 2022, available at https://socialwelfare.library.vcu.edu/ religious/ the-oneida-community-1848-1880-a-utopian-community/.

Opie, Kit Christopher, 'Monogamy and Infanticide in Complex Societies', Vol. 45, *Dunbar's Number*, April 2019.

'Plea for Marriage Equality', scobserver.in, 10 July 2024, available at https:// www. scobserver.in/cases/plea-for-marriage-equality/.

'Polygamy and Polygamous Marriages in India: An In-depth Look into Practices and Legal Framework', Centurylawfirm.in, available at https://www. centurylawfirm.in/ blog/polygamy-and-polygamous-marriages-in-india-an-in-depth-look-into-practices-and-legal-framework/.

Ray, S., 'The Glorious Rise & Scandalous Fall of "Sex Guru" Osho', *The Quint*, 9 April 2018.

Rivollat, M., Rohrlach, A.B., Ringbauer, H. *et al.*'Extensive pedigrees reveal the Social Organization of a Neolithic community', Vol. 620, No. 7974, *Nature*, 26 July 2023.

Sami, Waleed, 'Polarization and Division in India: A Nation at Crossroads', *Policy Wire*, 5 November 2024.

Scheidel, Walter, 'A peculiar institution?: Greco–Roman Monogamy in Global Context', Vol. 14, Issue 3, *The History of the Family*, 25 August 2009.

Singh, Madhur, 'Why Are Hindu Honor Killings Rising in India?', *Time*, 25 May 2010.

Small, Meredith F., Abbas, 'How Many Fathers Are Best?', *Discover Magazine*, 1 April 2003.

Starweather, Kathrine, 'Exploration into Human Polyandry: An Evolutionary Examination of the Non-Classical Cases', digitalcommons.unl.edu, 30 August 2010, available at chrome-extension://efaidnbmnnnibpcajpcglclefindmkaj/ https://digitalcommons.unl.edu/cgi/viewcontent.cgi?article=1005&context=a nthrotheses.

Tamera.org

Unni, K. Raman, 'Polyandry in Malabar', Vol. 7, No. 1, *Sociological Bulletin*, March 1958.

Verma, Lalmani, 'Activity of Anti-Romeo squads increased in last 5 yrs: Govt data', *The Indian Express*, 26 January 2023.